D1329964

Form 178 rev. 1-94

# Good Governance in
# Central and Eastern Europe

# ECONOMIES AND SOCIETIES IN TRANSITION

**General Editor: Ronald J. Hill**
*Professor of Comparative Government
and Fellow of Trinity College
Dublin, Ireland*

Economies and Societies in Transition is an important series which applies academic analysis and clarity of thought to the recent traumatic events in Eastern and Central Europe. As many of the preconceptions of the past half century are cast aside, newly independent and autonomous sovereign states are being forced to address long-term organic problems which had been suppressed by, or appeased within, the Communist system of rule.

The series is edited under the sponsorship of Lorton House, an independent charitable association which exists to promote the academic study of communism and related concepts.

# Good Governance in Central and Eastern Europe

## The Puzzle of Capitalism by Design

*Edited by*

## Herman W. Hoen

*Professor of International Political Economy, University of Groningen, The Netherlands*

ECONOMIES AND SOCIETIES IN TRANSITION

**Edward Elgar**
Cheltenham, UK • Northampton, MA, USA

Published by
Edward Elgar Publishing Limited
Glensanda House
Montpellier Parade
Cheltenham
Glos GL50 1UA
UK

Edward Elgar Publishing, Inc.
136 West Street
Suite 202
Northampton
Massachusetts 01060
USA


A catalogue record for this book
is available from the British Library


**Library of Congress Cataloguing in Publication Data**

Good governance in Central and Eastern Europe : the puzzle of capitalism by design / edited by Herman W. Hoen.
       p. cm. — (Economies and societies in transition)
    Includes bibliographical references and index.
    1. Europe, Central—Economic conditions—1989- 2. Corporate governance—
Europe, Central. 3. Europe, Central—Politics and government—1989- 4.
Europe, Eastern—Economic conditions—1989- 5. Corporate governance—
Europe, Eastern. 6. Europe, Eastern—Politics and government—1989- I. Hoen,
Herman Willem, 1960- II. Series.

HC244 .G6 2001
338.947—dc21
                                                                           2001023911
ISBN 1 84064 618 7

Printed and bound in Great Britain by Bookcraft (Bath) Ltd

# Contents

# Tables

# Figures

# Abbreviations

| | |
|---|---|
| CDU | Christian Democratic Union [Germany] |
| CEE | Central and Eastern Europe |
| CIS | Commonwealth of Independent States |
| CSP | country strategy paper |
| EBRD | European Bank for Reconstruction and Development |
| ECU | European Currency Unit |
| EFF | Extended Fund Facility [International Monetary Fund] |
| EFTA | European Free Trade Association |
| EIB | European Investment Bank |
| EMU | European Monetary Union |
| EU | European Union |
| FDI | foreign direct investment |
| FYROM | Former Yugoslav Republic of Macedonia |
| GDP | gross domestic product |
| GDR | German Democratic Republic |
| GKO | treasury bills [Russian Federation] |
| HRD | human resource development |
| HZDS | Movement for a Democratic Slovakia |
| IDS | Institute of Development Studies |
| IFI | international financial institution |
| IMF | International Monetary Fund |
| MOF | Ministry of Finance |
| NATO | North Atlantic Treaty Organisation |
| NGO | non-government organisation |
| NIR | national institutional review |
| OECD | Organisation for Economic Co-operation and Development |
| OFZ | longer-dated coupon-bearing bonds [Russian Federation] |
| PDS | Party of Democratic Socialism [Germany] |
| PHARE | Poland and Hungary: Aid for the Reconstruction of Economies [European Union] |
| PSC | post-socialist country |
| SAL | structural adjustment loan [World Bank] |
| SBA | standby agreement [International Monetary Fund] |
| SD | Party of the Democratic Left [Slovakia] |
| SDK | Slovak Democratic Coalition [Slovakia] |

| SECAL | sectoral adjustment loan [World Bank] |
| SMK | Party of the Hungarian Coalition [Slovakia] |
| SNS | Slovak National Party |
| SOP | Party of Civic Understanding [Slovakia] |
| SPD | Social Democratic Party [Germany] |
| STASI | state security police [German Democratic Republic] |
| STF | Systemic Transformation Fund [International Monetary Fund] |
| TACIS | Technical Assistance for the Commonwealth of Independent States [European Union] |
| UNDP | United Nations Development Programme |
| USAID | United States Agency for International Development |
| USSR | Union of Soviet Socialist Republics |

# Notes on Contributors

Joachim Ahrens is a lecturer in economics at the University of Göttingen (Germany), where he also received his PhD. He is an expert in development economics and has published numerous articles in this field. He is particularly interested in the extent to which international financial institutions influence long-term development in less-developed and former socialist countries. In 1998, he worked for several months at the Asian Development Bank in Manila (The Philippines).

David L. Bartlett is International Development Consultant and was visiting professor of Political Sciences at Yerevan Sate University (Armenia). He is the author of *The Political Economy of Dual Transformations: Market Reform and Democratization in Hungary* (University of Michigan Press, 1997) and winner of the 1998 Edward A. Hewett Prize for Political Economy of the American Association for the Advancement of Slavic Studies. He has published numerous articles and book chapters on financial reforms, privatisation and foreign investment in Eastern Europe and the former Soviet Union.

Hans-J. Giessmann is a Senior Researcher at the Institute for Peace Research and Security Policy at the University of Hamburg (Germany). Also, he is Associate Professor of Political Sciences at the University of Hamburg. He holds PhD degrees in Philosophy and in Political Science. His major research topics are European security politics; global security issues and arms control, disarmament and arms production, exports and conversion. He publishes frequently on these subjects. Among his latest works are 'The Cocooned Giant: Germany and European Security', *Hamburger Beiträge zur Friedensforschung und Sicherheitspolitik* (September 1999) and *Handbook of Security 1997/1998. Security in Central Europe and NATO Enlargement* (1997).

Oleh Havrylyshyn is Canadian and was born in 1943. He received his PhD in 1972 from the Massachusetts Institute of Technology. He was Special Advisor/Deputy Minister of Finance in the Government of Ukraine in 1992 and Alternate Executive Director in the IMF's Executive Board during 1993–96. He joined the staff of the IMF in 1996 as Assistant Director in the Policy Development and Review Department. Since 1997 he has been Senior Advisor in the IMF's European II Department and is dealing with Fund operations in the Baltic countries, Russia and other countries of the former Soviet Union.

Karen Henderson is a lecturer in East European politics at the University of Leicester (United Kingdom). She has published extensively on politics and democi..isation in post-communist societies. With Neil Robinson she co-authored *Post-communist Politics: An Introduction*, which standard reference was published by Prentice Hall in 1997. Currently, she is also working on the topic of eastward enlargement of the European Union. She edited *Back to Europe: Central and Eastern Europe and the European Union* (1999), published by UCL press in London.

Herman W. Hoen holds a chair as professor in International Political Economy at the University of Groningen (The Netherlands). He wrote a PhD on Hungarian export performance in the 1970s and 1980s. His current research focuses on economic transformation from a centrally planned to a market economy. His monograph on this theme, *The Transformation of Economic systems in Central Europe*, was published by Edward Elgar (1998).

Ivailo Izvorski was born in 1966 in Bulgaria. He received his PhD in economics from Yale University in 1997. In 1996 he joined the IMF as an economist in the Research Department and during 1997–99 he worked in the IMF's European II Department on Belarus and Turkmenistan. Since June 1999, he has been affiliated to the Institute of International Finance, where he works as an economist focusing on Bulgaria, Hungary and the Baltic states.

Ian Jeffries is a lecturer in the Centre of Russian and East European Studies at the University of Wales (Swansea). He is one of the most productive writers in the field of political and economic transformation in Central and Eastern Europe. His publications include *Socialist Economies and the Transition to the Market: A Guide* (1993), *A Guide to the Economies in Transition* (1996) and, together with Robert Bideleux, *A History of Eastern Europe: Crisis and Change* (1998), all published by Routledge.

Ron van Rooden is Dutch and was born in 1963. In 1988 he graduated in economics at Erasmus University in Rotterdam (The Netherlands). During 1988–94 he worked as an economist in the Domestic Research and Monetary and Economic Policy Department of De Nederlandsche Bank (Dutch Central Bank). Since May 1994, he has worked as an economist in the IMF's European II Department focusing on Azerbaijan, Ukraine and Moldova.

# Acknowledgements

The subtitle of this volume on 'good governance' in Central and Eastern Europe is 'The Puzzle of Capitalism by Design'. It underlines the intertwining of political and economic transformation in Central and Eastern Europe during the last decade. Autonomous economic transformation does not exist. It depends on political decisions and is, therefore, vulnerable to the process of democratisation. Since the collapse of communism in 1989, the Central and Eastern European region has witnessed fascinating transformation policies. The implementation of a democratic order embedded in a market economy environment proved difficult and was subject to tremendous variety within the region. Different strategies were applied and where policies were similar, performances diverged repeatedly, as what was suitable for one country proved inappropriate for another.

None the less, there was common ground. By and large, communism did not return. At times (former) communists reappeared within the political arena, but none had either the willingness or the capability to reverse the path set after the revolution of 1989. From the point of view of the theory of political economy, the unquestionable desire to transform both the political and the economic systems far from self-evident: on the contrary, democratisation and market reform have often been perceived as contradictory. The question then is: 'How can good governance be secured?' This turned out to be a complicated jigsaw puzzle.

I am extremely grateful to the contributors of this volume for their willingness to tackle this issue with their own particular knowledge and I have enjoyed working and collaborating with them. Working with them also made me aware that the impossibility of editing a book in solitary confinement changes to a joy when collaborating with a group of such inspiring authors. I felt truly honoured to co-operate with Joachim Ahrens, David L. Bartlett, Hans-J. Giessmann, Oleh Havrylyshyn, Karen Henderson, Ivailo Izvorski, Ian Jeffries and Ron van Rooden. But in completing this book, I am indebted to many others as well.

First of all, I am very grateful to the 'Centre for European Security Studies' (CESS) in Groningen, whose director, Peter Volten, took the initiative for organising the conference 'Taking Stock on Transformation'. The conference proved a great success. In the spring of 1999, the participants were hosted in the city of Groningen in the Netherlands; discussions were held in the field of transforming civil military relations, the role of non-governmental organisations in democratic reform and the international dimension of transformation. The latter topic was worked out as the subject for this volume. I would like to thank Margriet Drent, David Greenwood, Sipke de Hoop, Sander Huisman, Tanya Kolosova, Koen Marquering, Elzaline Schraa and Peter Volten, who have been patient CESS collaborators and have helped me complete the editing of this volume based on their in-house publication, the *Harmonie Paper*.

Second, I feel indebted to all the participants of the conference organised by CESS, in particular to Frank Bönker of the 'Frankfurt Institute of Transformation Studies' (Frankfurt/Oder), Pál Dunay of the 'Geneva Centre for Security Studies' (Geneva) and Michael Mihalka of the 'George C. Marshall Center for Security Studies' (Garmisch Partenkirchen). They have been extremely helpful in improving the arguments of the chapters during discussions in Groningen. But, of course, the usual disclaimer applies: they are in no way to be held responsible for any error, omission or inaccurate conclusion. This also holds for Heinrich Vogel of the 'Federal Institute for Russian, East European and International Studies' (Cologne), who is one of the intellectual instigators of this book's subject and who agreed to chair some of the discussions which ultimately led to this volume; unfortunately, he was unable to join the CESS conference.

Finally, I am very grateful to Ron Hill of Trinity College (Dublin), who was willing to read and comment on the entire manuscript in a very short period of time.

Herman W. Hoen
Groningen, February 2001

# 1. Taking Stock on Transformation: Market Reform and Democratisation in Central and Eastern Europe

## Herman W. Hoen

### TEN YEARS AFTER: IS THERE LIGHT AT THE END OF THE TUNNEL?

The transformation in Central and Eastern Europe from a politically authoritarian system with mandatory economic planning to a democratic order based on market co-ordination has presented one of the major challenges in contemporary history. In order to fulfil these tasks, there were no historical precedents to rely upon, nor were there clear-cut conceptual frameworks to underpin these dual transformations.[1] Concerning Central and Eastern Europe, scholars seem to have been confused time and again. In retrospect, of course, all tend to present the facts so as to confirm their own theories, but two aspects should not be overlooked.

First, there is no well-attested evidence of any forecast regarding the collapse of the communist system. On the contrary, discussions of the existence and feasibility of a socialist economic order were closed several decades ago.[2] No matter precisely how and in what format, economic co-ordination by means of central planning simply existed. It was referred to as 'real existing socialism'. The system had its advantages and its disadvantages and the prevailing view was that it needed to be 'reformed' rather than 'transformed'. After all, communism and its concomitant organisation of central planning had an outstanding reputation in terms of stability.

Second, once the curtain fell in December 1989, nobody really knew how to cope with the transformation. As van Brabant put it, 'they [economists] know next to nothing about undoing the planning environment and coming to grips with the wide-ranging legacies of the earlier communist dominance in societal affairs'[3] Mainstream concepts failed, since within these concepts institutions are perceived as constant. It is acknowledged that institutional data do have an impact on economic performance, but they are in no way

1

subject to change. In other words, institutions are not explicitly taken into account. That also holds for the most important institution, the market itself, which is assumed to function relatively well. Consequently, on the basis of these analyses it is difficult to underpin theoretically the creation of markets. Transformation, however, impinges on the change of institutions, not so much on the effect of a given economic order on its performance.

The absence of historical precedents and theoretical tools led to a broad palette of transformation policies applied in Central and Eastern Europe from the beginning of the 1990s. Besides, despite great similarities in communist dictatorship, the political and economic legacy varied enormously among the countries facing the tasks of transformation. As a result, different strategies emerged and, where policies were similar, performances diverged. Apparently, what was suitable for one country proved inappropriate for another. There was, however, one common denominator in the transformation experience. All Central and Eastern European countries faced a large contraction in economic activity at the beginning of the transformation. What came to be known as the 'transformation crisis' was much deeper and lasted much longer than expected. The idea that under central planning there was a large amount of output that only existed on paper did not really alter this view. The extent to which 'output that was not' induced a nominal overestimation of economic decline appeared to be a minor short-term problem. The fundamental problem of the former regime was the 'output that was, but should not have been'[4] A lot of what was produced under central planning appeared to be obsolete in a market environment. Therefore, production had to be restructured.

It goes without saying that some countries have proved to be more successful in regaining economic growth than others. But ten years after the collapse of communism, only Poland and Slovenia surpassed the 1989 gross domestic product (GDP) level. The Czech Republic, initially tagged the 'brightest pupil in class', appeared to suffer a crisis and did not reach the magic marker. At the celebration of the second quinquennium, Hungary, which during the communist era became known as the 'brightest shed in the camp', was also performing at a level of economic activity below that of 1989.[5] The further East one observed the situation, the more dismal the picture. For example, in many countries of the Commonwealth of Independent States (CIS), the level of economic activity was less than half of that in 1989. Russia, being the largest country of the CIS, fitted into this gloomy pattern. On top of that, the rouble crisis which emerged in the summer of 1998 had a dramatic effect upon the economic performance of 1999, which again showed a decline of approximately 5 per cent of Russian GDP. Ten years after the collapse of communism, there appeared to be light at the end of the tunnel for most of the Central and Eastern European

countries. But for quite a number of them, it was the light of an oncoming train.

Now the question is: 'why was the transformation so cumbersome?' Many authors stressed the fact that the transformation to a democratic order based upon market co-ordination was too encompassing. Indeed, a huge number of demanding reforms had to be carried out, such as macroeconomic stabilisation, liberalisation of prices, production and trade, microeconomic restructuring and, last but not least, institutional reforms to underpin the rules of the market game. The authors adducing this argument focus upon speed and sequencing of reforms.[6] But even in the (hypothetical) case in which one is able to minimise the costs of transformation by calculating the speed and sequencing of reforms, the question remains: 'is one politically able to implement the reforms at the desired time and speed?'

This observation triggered an approach in the tradition of political economy. Most of the authors who follow this line of thought address the problematic relation between democratisation on the one hand and market reform on the other. The argument is that democracy might impede implementation of the economic reforms enumerated above, since these will necessarily have distributional welfare effects. Therefore, there should be a minimal level of economic development in order to have democratisation and market economic reform coincide successfully.[7] Others have emphasised the argument of political credit during the period immediately following the revolution. This view implies that for a limited period, policy makers could apply some kind of 'scorched-earth policy', since the former regime can be held responsible for the negative welfare consequences of transformation.[8] Finally, it has been argued that democratisation facilitated rather than impeded market reforms in Central and Eastern Europe. According to the proponents of this line of thought, there was continuing political intermediation during communism, which settled distributional conflicts. The revolution of 1989, therefore, heralded not only the end of communism itself, but also the end of political influence in the field of economic regulation.[9]

This book examines the transformation processes in Central and Eastern Europe and builds on the arguments put forward in the tradition of political economy. Its basic assumptions are that designing a market economy is not to be mistaken for destroying the institutional legacy of communism – a market order is not the negation of central planning – and that mutual dependency between democratisation and market reform has a definite impact on the path of transformation. In other words, economic systems are understood as irreversible and path-dependent. One cannot simply dismantle the former regime, and each step in the reform process influences the set of alternatives for the reforms that still need to be implemented. The legacy of the past is decisive. This is not to deny that the success or failure of transformation depends largely on the policies applied, but that the extent to which these appropriate policies were feasible is pivotal.

In the remainder of this chapter, the validity and the consequences of these assumptions are further addressed. The following section is theoretical in nature. It centres on the (political) motives for and the impediments to market reforms. The leading thread is the political likelihood of transformation based upon assumptions of economic behaviour. Subsequently, the arguments turn to the issues of institutional change and 'good governance' and the extent to which they can be furthered by external conditionality and by domestic political forces. In the concluding section, the outline of the remainder of the book is sketched.

## A POLITICAL ECONOMY OF TRANSFORMATION

This section addresses the process of transformation from a centrally planned to a market economy within the framework of political economy. As stated above, mainstream economics – neoclassical economics – does not really suffice to underpin theoretically the transformation, because it considers institutions as data. What matters is not so much the fact that institutions affect economic performance, but that institutions are subject to change. Now the question is: 'what is the probability that they will change and converge to market institutions?' This question goes well beyond pure economics. Leaving aside the problem that the desired order is far from clear to those responsible for reform, a political economic theory has to focus upon the problem of how to accomplish a new economic order from a given situation. This is not a completely untrodden field for economists, though the purpose has always been to conceive policy targets within a given economic order, rather than to contrive transformation targets and instruments, that is, the conversion of one economic order to another.

We shall not refute the basic assumptions of neoclassical economics, of which those presuming the rational behaviour of utility-maximising agents are the pivotal ones, but gratefully make use of the politico-economic theories that gained momentum in the 1960s and 1970s. These complemented neoclassical thinking and have put forward the idea that government policy is to be explained in terms of mutual exchange between the targets and the behaviour of civilians, civil servants and politicians.[10] All these actors will try to maximise utility, which may result in a suboptimal outcome at the macro level. Now, which instruments are at the disposal of reformers for the implementation of institutional change? Regarding economic reforms in the 1970s and 1980s, it was legitimate to ask why, for example, in Hungary, during the stage of a one-party system in which relations between the party and the other institutions were so unambiguously set, final results of economic reform deviated to such a large extent from the targets set by the Communist Party. Regarding economic transformation in the 1990s, the search for policy instruments, and the (economic) interests they might serve, is simply indispensable.

There are good arguments for regarding market reform as a collective good. Non-exclusiveness and non-rivalry are the two characteristics of these commodities. The first implies that no one can be excluded from using it, whereas the latter points to the fact that individual use of the commodity does not diminish total stocks available. If this is the case, nobody is willing to pay a positive market price. Although there are not as many collective goods as one is initially inclined to believe, transformation seems to fulfil the conditions for such a good. A market economy provides freedom of contract, guarantees competition and facilitates legal opportunities to enforce obedience to the rules. It is available to all (non-exclusive) and the use being made of the market rules does not limit the possibility of other users (non-rivalry). Textbook economics tells us that in order to have the public good one needs a special body to provide it, though not necessarily a government agency.[11] The fact that transformation can be seen as a public good makes it unlikely to emerge.

What is at stake here is the argument of external effects. As in the case of growth theory and technological change, it can be stated that what is beneficial to one is beneficial to all. From the assumption that transformation is a public good it follows that the problem of free-riding has to be faced. If all individuals want to have a free ride, transformation may never be achieved. In other words, it needs to be organised, that is, 'governed'.

The behaviour of individuals in groups is crucial. In this respect, an illuminating point of view can be found in interest-group theory.[12] One of the implicit assumptions in this theory is that some groups are perfectly able to look after their interests, while other groups are not. It implies that eventually an unbalanced power structure will emerge. Mancur Olson played a pioneering role in the debate on organisation of collective interests. He concluded that the size of a group is decisive in determining the extent to which an organisation is successful. In small groups, individual effort is perceived as necessary for achieving the common interest. The individual contribution is not felt in large groups and, therefore, free-riding endangers the common interest.[13]

A classic example of undesired interest structures is the case of tariffs. For the society as a whole, the imposition of trade restrictions is detrimental to welfare. Producers in the respective industry, however, may benefit substantially. In other words, the costs are spread over a large number of people and evoke only minor protests, while the benefits flow to a small well-identified number.[14] The individual's decision to join a group or not is supposed to be rational and in accordance with his or her own interest.

According to Olson's subsequent publications on interest-group behaviour as an explanation for economic growth and stagnation, an important constraint in generating economic growth is deployed by so-called distributional coalitions.[15] These are interest groups which try to change the income distribution to their members' benefit.[16] Instead of contributing to an increase in total income, distributional coalitions attempt to have a larger share of a given quantity of welfare, which phenomenon is the classic example of rent seeking. Besides distributional coalitions, encompassing organisations are identified.[17] When looking after their interests, encompassing interest groups take note of the impact of their activities on national welfare. Not only the division but also the growth of income is considered important to these groups.

Theories of interest-group behaviour have been applied predominantly to market economies. Since perceived undesirable regulation assumes market intervention, it is obvious that attention has been restricted to this economic order.[18] Application of interest-group theories to centrally planned economies appeared only after the collapse of communism and all the studies focused upon the Soviet Union and on classic mandatory planning rather than on parametric planning, as was applied in Hungary since 1968 and in Poland from 1982.[19] The successful period of vast economic growth in the Soviet Union (1950–65) is explained in terms of leadership. One could even speak of a pure property rights approach, that is, by assuming Stalin to be the owner of the Soviet Union. During this period, Soviet society was within the competence of very few. Their political fate was largely dependent upon the well-being of the community. This line of thought follows a cost–benefit analysis. There was a small group, which had encompassing interests. The decline of the Soviet Union begins with the Brezhnev era. Gradually an unbalanced interest structure emerged. Ministries and enterprises became indispensable agents in supplying information to the planning authorities. They behaved as distributional coalitions and 'institutional sclerosis' crept in.

The theory has been applied only marginally to the transformation processes in Central and Eastern Europe. This is predominantly due to the theoretical flaws. There are many objections to the theory, ranging from mono-causality to the point that the theory is hard to formalise mathematically. In the context of this chapter, two flaws will be mentioned. First of all, certain aspects of the behaviour of groups cannot be explained in terms of rational economic calculation. Many organisations hold broader interests and are not purely economically motivated. Classic examples are solidarity movements, where members do not have a direct interest in the achievement of the organisation's goal. But there are other examples as well. For instance, why would one consider going to a polling station and voting for a new president or parliament? The probability that one's vote is decisive is negligible. None the less, many make the effort and do vote. Considering the revolution of 1989 in Central and Eastern Europe, the case is even clearer. The decision to join demonstrations against the communist rulers, for example in Dresden, was a risky venture and could coincide with high costs. At the same time, the expected marginal effect of the individual demonstrator was practically zero. The individual costs were clear, whereas the individual benefits were difficult to identify. So, why not have a 'free lunch'?[20] It can be concluded for this critical notion on rationality that the theory is not able to explain the emergence of Solidarity (Poland) or Civic Forum (Czechoslovakia). The criticism of the assumption of rationality essentially lays bare the fact that the theory of interest groups is much better equipped to clarify a status quo than the dynamics of system switches. It underlines the improbability of market reform, whereas in Central and Eastern Europe the opposite could be observed.

The second flaw in Olson's interest-group theory is that it does not acknowledge the role of leadership in the accomplishment of collective goods.[21] This point is not an attack on the assumption of rationality, but focuses on the fact that some individuals perform the role of a kind 'Schumpeterian' entrepreneur. Individuals may have different time perspectives. Certain individuals may perceive it as an investment to step forward and take the initiative in organising and defending the interests of a group. This implies that – taking group interests into account – they accept that the individual commitment may be very large, but individual benefits may emerge later. These exceed the gains for the group as a whole and, therefore, are worth the effort. In the context of Central and Eastern Europe one might take political leadership of former opposition figures like Václav Havel as an example. Once the group interests are realised, these 'entrepreneurs' become likely candidates for high political positions, such as a presidency. It has to be added that the individual benefit has to be calculated not only in income, but also in prestige.

## THE 'G-WORDS': EXTERNAL AND INTERNAL PRESSURE TO REFORM

Despite these theoretical drawbacks, there are still good reasons to study the transformation in Central and Eastern Europe from the perspective of interest-group theory. As noted, the second theoretical flaw can easily be perceived as a complement to rather than as a refutation of the pivotal idea. Moreover, the fact that, according to the theory, what happened in Central and Eastern Europe was unlikely to happen – coincidence of democratisation and market reform – makes it extremely interesting to investigate what conditions should be fulfilled to avoid free-riding and to examine the extent to which these have been fulfilled in the region. Despite the fact that there were many failures during the transformation processes, it has to be stressed again that there has been a return of communists, but not of communism. It is a search for 'good governance': a policy which defends the interests of the society at large and not necessarily the particular interests of small groups.

Several types of control can prevent free-riding behaviour. This is the problem of governance. First, one can apply 'selective incentives'. Those who are not willing to pay will not benefit. For the idea of achieving transformation as a collective good, selective incentives are somewhat problematic, since by definition a public good is non-exclusive. The obvious example is the membership of labour unions. But there are numerous other examples. An alternative can be found in the solution of what is known as 'voluntary coercion'. There are many instances of this option. The best known is the forced membership of labour unions in order to benefit from the their achievements, which is also a valid argument for transformation. Those who share a common interest are willing to accept forced membership of a group, since they acknowledge the danger of free-riding.

The concept of 'voluntary coercion' highlights the role of international organisations as key actors. In a broad perspective, one can perceive a mutual dependency between integration with the West and transformation from a centrally planned to a market economy in Central and Eastern Europe. On the one hand, continuing reforms will expedite the process of integration. On the other hand, integration in the West can be seen as a stick, which can be used to implement necessary but painful economic reforms. Once the perspective on integration in the West is perceived as real, there will be political willingness to co-operate and reform. More specifically, this argument focuses upon the role of international organisations and the extent to which they are able to enforce 'good governance'.

Second, and this acknowledges the theoretical flaw of leadership mentioned in the previous section, there might be individuals willing to do more than their fair share. Thus, one might wonder why certain individuals are willing to step forward and become leaders of political organisations. In the foregoing section it has been pointed out that policy is the ultimate outcome of interplay between a large number of actors, among which the government is only one. A government may be forced by international organisations to apply sound policies, but, of course, other actors must not be neglected. Within the context of the political economy of transformation sketched above, it is particularly interesting to know whether leaders emerge to support market reform that may go beyond particular interests. What is the role of elites, how do they emerge and, most importantly, in what ways are they able to influence governance?

The classic dichotomy is that of 'power elites' versus 'pluralism'.[22] The famous concept of C. Wright Mills's power elites is rather static however, and focuses on agreement rather than disagreement among different organisations and groups in society, be they military, political or economic.

The view implies that interests coincide and that there is, by and large, agreement on how to see national goals and concomitant policies.[23] The concept of pluralism is definitely not conducive to consensus among different groups in society.[24] There are different fields of expertise, different interests, and, therefore, a huge variety of opinions and unpredictable policy outcomes. The latter concept is more in line with the assumptions of maximising behaviour of rational agents and, therefore, better fits into the approach outlined above.

Both 'voluntary coercion' and 'leadership' as the two options to combat free-rider behaviour will be examined in this book. Both focus on what might be referred to as the 'G-words' in transformation: good governance. For the sake of clarity, it is stressed once more that good governance was not the self-evident policy in the region. However, it is assumed that those countries which applied a transformation policy that served the interests of society at large, performed better than those of distributional coalitions.

## OUTLINE OF THE BOOK

This book scrutinises the 'G-words' in the process of political and economic transformation in Central and Eastern Europe. As emphasised above, there is no such thing as naturalness of market reform and democratisation. Much depends on 'good governance' and the crucial question is: 'how to promote and enforce it?' In the remaining chapters, three aspects will receive attention: (i) economic performance and 'good governance', (ii) external conditionality and 'good governance' and (iii) elite formation and domestic constraints on 'good governance'.

Firstly, we are interested in the extent to which economic performance is attributable to 'good governance'. In Chapter 2, Ian Jeffries presents an overview of the topic. He focuses on developments in Russia up to the 'rouble crisis' in 1998 and lays bare the vulnerability of sound economic policy. The research is restricted to Russia, but Jeffries's contribution is also valid when applied to other countries in which the implementation of a market economy embedded in a democratic order has been given top priority on the political agenda. In Chapter 3, Oleh Havrylyshyn, Ivailo Izvorski and Ron van Rooden seek statistical evidence regarding the relation between economic performance and 'good governance'. They address macro-economic performance in Central and Eastern Europe and search for the extent to which success can be ascribed to different policies of stabilisation and liberalisation. The chapter notes the tension between 'initial conditions' and 'good governance'. The authors conclude that stabilisation and appropriate reform strategies rather than initial conditions are the key to economic growth. In that respect, they are at variance with, for example,

Coricelli, who says that 'the impact of liberalisation becomes statistically insignificant when indicators of initial conditions ... are included'.[25]

Having underscored the importance of 'good governance' in these chapters, we shift the focus to the question of how to promote and enforce it. The role of international organisations comes to the fore in this respect. What counts is the challenge of anchoring reforms. Clearly, the prospect of becoming a member of the European Union (EU) helps to create domestic political credit in order to implement painful but necessary reforms. In this volume, however, we gauge not only the impact of the EU, but also the conditionality provisions imposed by international financial institutions (IFIs) such as the International Monetary Fund (IMF), the World Bank and the European Bank for Reconstruction and Development (EBRD). In Chapter 4, Joachim Ahrens addresses the issue of 'good governance' and conditionality. He presents an in-depth analysis of the different perceptions IFIs have of 'good governance', criticises the *ad hoc* manner in which these multilateral organisations often carry out their tasks in this respect and, in discussing the possibility of a new kind of conditionality in international lending operations, queries the (lack of) political mandate of the IFIs. Ahrens suggests a 'focal-point approach'. By concentrating on 'governance' in reforming national banking and the ministry of finance, government agencies for competition and anti-trust policy, and, finally, education and training, there may arise crucial spin-off effects. This author also makes a strong plea for matching the level of government representation in the negotiations between lender and borrower.

The subsequent chapter by David L. Bartlett also addresses conditionality. Bartlett stresses the fact that for the countries in Central and Eastern Europe stabilisation is no longer the main issue. In line with the thrust of Ahrens's chapter, he signals a strong need for 'good governance' in continuing microeconomic reform. The implementation of a well-functioning market economy is too often mistaken for decentralisation of economic decision-making. But destroying the legacy of central planning is not enough. The rules of the market game have to be implemented and complied with. Therefore, conditionality and 'good governance' should be applied at the level of courts of justice and the civil service. Bartlett also foresees a changing division of labour between functional international organisations, the IMF and the World Bank, and regional international organisations – like the EU – to the benefit of the latter.

Chapters 6 and 7 focus upon the third aspect of 'good governance' under scrutiny in this book: elite formation. Karen Henderson looks at the role of elites in the transformation in the Czech and Slovak Republics, describes their agendas in these countries and tries to explain why, despite a perceived common background, the elites appeared to be so different. She elucidates the contrast between Czech 'consensus' and Slovak 'polarisation' in terms of what she refers to as 'geographic', 'ethnic', and 'political divides'. What becomes clear is twofold. First, the elites in Czechoslovakia were far from homogeneous, and, second, the prospects for 'good governance' by elites in Slovakia are not as gloomy as frequently presented in the literature.

Whereas Henderson is basically discussing a transformation as a result of the break-up of a country, in the concluding chapter, Hans-J. Giessmann describes the role of elites in a transformation characterised by a merger – the German case. This experience nearly fulfilled the desperate desire of scholars in the political and social sciences to have a laboratory experiment. The German case would answer the question: 'what does a transformation from an authoritarian system with mandatory planning to a market economy embedded in a democratic political order actually cost?' To find that crucial answer, look at the bill for the 'foster parents'. The transformation-by-merger showed that the costs were extremely high indeed. It also showed, however, that even for the most prosperous among the former communist countries the bill has not been entirely paid yet, since problems are far from being settled. Giessmann provides us with an analysis of the East German elites, the vacuum in which they were lost after rigorous removal of the old guard and the problems they have in positioning themselves *vis-à-vis* the 'Wessies'. It is a convincing proof of the argument that the design of capitalism is more than a painstaking completion of a jigsaw.

## NOTES

1. The phrase, 'dual transformations' underlines the fact that, since the collapse of communism, both a political and an economic transformation were set in motion. The term is borrowed from David L. Bartlett, *The Political Economy of Dual Transformations: Market Reform and Democratization in Hungary* (Ann Arbor 1997).
2. See Marie Lavigne, *The Economics of Transition: From Socialist Economy to Market Economy* (Basingstoke 1999); Hans-Jürgen Wagener, *Zur Analyse von Wirtschaftssystemen. Eine Einführung* (Berlin 1979).
3. Jozef M. van Brabant, 'Lessons from the Wholesale Transformation in the East', *Comparative Economic Studies*, 35 (1993) pp. 80–81.
4. Jan Winiecki, 'Heterodox Stabilisation in Eastern Europe', EBRD Working Paper, 8, European Bank for Reconstruction and Development (London 1993). The necessity of the crisis is well documented. See, for example, Lavigne, *The Economic of Transition*, pp. 150–61; Michael Bruno, 'Stabilization and Reform in Eastern Europe after Communism', *IMF Staff Paper*, 39 (1992) pp. 319–47; Holger Schmieding, "From Plan to Market: On the Nature of the Transformation Crisis', *Weltwirtschaftliches Archiv*, 129, 2 (1993) pp. 216–53.
5. For GDP levels, see European Bank for Reconstruction and Development, Transition Report (London various years). See Herman W. Hoen, *The Transformation of Economic Systems in Central Europe* (Cheltenham 1998) on the misleading qualification of transformation strategies in the Czech Republic and Hungary.

6. Ibid., Chapter 1. The reader is also referred to, for example, Ben Slay, "Rapid versus Gradual Economic Transition", *Radio Free Europe/ Radio Liberty Report*, 3 (1994) pp. 31–42; Peter Murrell, "Evolutionary and Radical Approaches to Economic Reform", *Economics of Planning*, 25 (1992) pp. 79–95.

7. See, for example, Claus Offe, 'Capitalism by Democratic Design? Democratic Theory Facing the Triple Transition in East Central Europe', *Social Research*, 58, 4 (1991) pp. 865–92; Adam Przeworski, *Democracy and the Market: Political and Economic Reforms in Eastern Europe and Latin America* (Cambridge 1991).

8. See Leszek Balcerowicz, *Socialism, Capitalism, Transformation* (Budapest 1995); Gerard Roland, 'The Role of Political Constraints in Transition Strategies', CEPR Discussion Paper, 943, Centre for Economic Policy Research (London 1994).

9. Bartlett, *The Political Economy of Dual Transformations*.

10. For an excellent overview, see Bruno S. Frey, *Modern Political Economy* (Oxford 1978).

11. This idea is borrowed from Frank Bönker, 'The Political Economy of Fiscal Reform in Eastern Europe', mimeo, Humboldt University (Berlin 1999).

12. See Thráinn Eggertsson, *Economic Behavior and Institutions* (Cambridge 1990) pp. 171–80.

13. Mancur Olson, *The Logic of Collective Action* (Cambridge MA 1965).

14. The example is taken from Anne O. Krueger, 'The Political Economy of a Rent-Seeking Society', *American Economic Review*, 64, 3 (1974) pp. 291–303.

15. Mancur Olson, *The Rise and Decline of Nations: Economic Growth, Stagflation and Social Rigidities* (New Haven 1982).

16. Ibid., pp. 43–7

17. Ibid., pp. 47–53.

18. For an overview, see Hoen, *The Transformation of Economic Systems in Central Europe*, pp. 164–6.

19. Peter Murell and Mancur Olson, 'The Devolution of Centrally Planned Economies', *Journal of Comparative Economics*, 15 (1991) pp. 239–65 and Mancur Olson, 'The Hidden Path to a Successful Economy', in Christopher Clague and Gordon C. Rausser (eds), *The Emergence of Market Economies in Eastern Europe* (Cambridge 1992) pp. 55–75.

20. There are numerous other examples. For an extensive list see Brian Barry and Russil Hardin (eds.), *Rational Man and Irrational Society: An Introduction and Source Book* (Beverly Hills 1982).

21. Norman Frohlich, Joe A. Oppenheimer and Oran R. Young, *Political Leadership and Collective Goods* (Princeton 1971).

22. See Bruce Russett and Harvey Starr, *World Politics; The Menu for Choice*, fifth edition (New York 1996) pp. 197–201.

23. C. Wright Mills, *The Power Elite* (New York 1956).

24. See Robert A. Dahl, *Who Governs? Democracy and Power in American Cities* (New Haven 1961).

25. Fabrizio Coricelli, *Macroeconomic Policies and Development of Markets in Transition Economies* (Budapest 1998) p. 34.

# 2. Good Governance and the First Decade of Transition: An Overview

## Ian Jeffries

### INTRODUCTION

What has happened over the last decade is truly remarkable, so much so that it is difficult to grasp the magnitude of the changes. Who foresaw that communism would collapse in Eastern Europe, let alone as early as late 1989? Even after this, the disintegration of the Soviet Union in late 1991 was still a shock, especially since it happened in a relatively peaceful fashion. The world has not stopped spinning. As the transitional economies have increasingly become integrated into the world economy, the costs as well as the benefits of globalisation have become all too apparent.[1]

It is also remarkable how quickly theorising about the transition has faded as regards 'big bang' or 'shock therapy' versus gradualism. My guess is that most people would agree that as much as possible should be done as quickly as possible. This, of course, presupposes many questions, and political as well as economic feasibility – in the context of the circumstances of individual countries – needs to be considered. The World Bank's conclusions are interesting: which works best, rapid or gradual reform? This question has no simple answer.[2]

A country's starting circumstances, both economic and political, greatly affect the range of reform policies and outcomes open to it. Within this range, however, the clear lesson of the past few years' reforms is that, regardless of the starting point, decisive and consistent reform pays off.[3] In every case [including China, which adopted gradual reform] what matters is the breadth of the policy reforms attempted and the consistency with which they are maintained.[4]

What is apparent empirically is that a broad dividing line can be drawn between (a) the countries of what may still usefully be defined as Eastern Europe and (b) those of the Commonwealth of Independent States (CIS). There are, of course, great contrasts within these broad categories (for example, poorly performing Albania and Serbia plus troubled Romania within the former). But clearly countries like Hungary and Poland stand out like beacons compared with Russia and Ukraine. Why is this so? What has this got to do with good governance?

The President of the World Bank, James Wolfensohn, provides a useful definition and explanation of the importance of good governance:

> Development ... requires good governance, meaning open, transparent, accountable public institutions. In a market economy, growth, if it is to be lasting, must be regulated not overregulated, but guided by public institutions and private professional conduct which establish a foundation of transparency and fairness in economic life. There is no substitute for this transparency. This means accessible courts, effective bankruptcy laws, sound securities and competition regimes, and strong anti-corruption policies ... Effective, accessible public institutions are not just conducive to but a necessary condition for stable growth ... Principles of integrity and accountability are equally important for the private sector ... A private investment bank ... recently highlighted corporate governance as a primary factor in its investment recommendations ... In a world that pivots on the speed and perceived credibility of information, journalists must be free to uncover market information, both good and bad, and stock exchanges must be able to provide data instantaneously ... Transparency in financial markets is central.[5]

## GOOD GOVERNANCE AND THE ASIAN/RUSSIAN FINANCIAL CRISIS

A recent aspect of globalisation is the turmoil in many emerging market economies (which include the transition economies). Mexico was hit in 1994, but attention has centred on events since July 1997 when the currency of Thailand came under speculative attack. The financial panic spread to other Asian countries (such as Indonesia). As regards the transition countries, why was Russia in particular devastated by the Asian financial crisis while Hungary and Poland, for instance, escaped relatively unscathed? What has this got to do with good governance?

In mid-August 1998 Russia itself actually became the cause of further financial turmoil. This happened despite the fact that Russia is now a minnow in world economic terms (although note should be taken of the problems of which exchange rate to use and of dealing with the black economy). Commentators noted:

> Russia's economy ... is about the size of Switzerland's.[6]

> It is easy to forget that Russia is a small economy, whose trade links with the West are tiny. Western Europe's exports to Russia, for example, account for well under 0.5 per cent of Gross Domestic Product (GDP). However, it is already clear that the impact of this crisis will be greatly disproportionate to Russia's size".[7]

The country now accounts for less than 1 per cent of global GDP; its entire federal budget is dwarfed by the size of military spending by the United States of America (US).[8]

The main point to make is that the countries most adversely affected suffer from *fundamental weaknesses*, which were cruelly exposed by Asian financial turmoil. Prominent among these is the phenomenon of 'crony capitalism', such as incestuous links between banks and 'their' companies in the allocation of capital funds. Let us analyse what has happened to Russia and in so doing bring in the question of good governance.

Ironically, Russia seemed to be turning the corner in 1997: the economy grew, although only barely, for the first time since 1989, inflation was modest (after hyperinflation in 1992), direct foreign investment was markedly higher than in 1996 and the balance of payments on current account was still in surplus. Thus it should not be forgotten that events outside Russia, including falling world market prices for oil and gas (which are vitally important exports), have played a part in its recent distress. The chilling effects of the Asian financial crisis were kept at bay in the autumn of 1997 and the spring of 1998, albeit at the expense of dramatic rises in interest rates. So what went wrong on 17 August 1998 when Russia defaulted on its domestic debt and was forced to allow the rouble to float? What are the fundamental weaknesses of the Russia economy, which have dramatically distanced it even further from the economies of, say, Hungary and Poland?

Russia's inability to raise sufficient tax revenue to finance the *central* (federal) government's essential activities is crucial to gaining an understanding of the crisis. On 23 June 1998 Sergei Kiriyenko (Prime Minister 23 March–3 August 1998) stated: If the state does not learn to collect taxes it will cease to exist. Anatoli Chubais had earlier (17 April 1997) thought likewise: Russia is experiencing a monstrous state budget crisis, whose parameters, if truth be told, call into question the ability of the state to perform its functions.[9];

The government is basically bankrupt. New York City collects more in municipal taxes than Russia collects federal taxes.[10]

Deputy Finance Minister Mikhail Kasyanov said Wednesday [10 February 1999] that the International Monetary Fund (IMF) wanted Russia to double its tax collection ...The IMF considers that the revenues of the federal budget should be 17 per cent to 18 per cent of GDP, said Mr Kasyanov.[11]

Russia's inability to collect taxes is rapidly becoming the greatest threat to its economic and political stability. The current government cannot raise the revenues needed to run a modern state. Since economic reforms began in 1992 federal tax revenues have fallen from about 18 per cent of Russia's GDP to less than 10 per cent in 1997 – compared with about 31 per cent in Austria, 27 per cent in Germany and 18 per cent in the US.[12]

A different model is now gaining currency among political and economic analysts, who say that Russia is in imminent danger of becoming a 'failed state', not breaking into pieces as the Soviet Union did in December 1991, but simply ceasing to function as a cohesive federal government.[13]

It is important to note the stress on the federal level.

The concern is not that the government does not collect enough taxes. In fact, it collected 32 per cent of Russia's GDP last year [1997], the same proportion that the United States does. The problem is rather that Russia has no actual tax system. In practice, taxation is a free negotiation between the ubiquitous tax inspectors and taxpayers, meaning that the strong win and small entrepreneurs are chased out of business. [14]

The problem is an arbitrary tax system, with excessively high rates and ruthless government officials ... The present system is so arbitrary that you are more likely to be forced to pay a penalty if you pay your taxes than if you ignore them altogether. Moreover, excessive rates make it impossible to collect taxes. Until recently penalties have been extraordinarily high and big enterprises presume they can be negotiated away ... Apparently many big companies enjoy immunity ... One serious problem is that taxes tend to stop at the regional level, where budgets are extremely wasteful.[15]

A budget deficit occurs when a government spends more than it raises in tax revenue. The size of the budget and the way it is financed have a crucial bearing on the control of inflation. The budget deficit can be financed by (i) increasing the money supply, (ii) borrowing from the private sector of the economy and/or from foreigners, or (iii) some combination of (i) and (ii). It is now the federal budget, rather than the consolidated state budget, which includes the regions, that is now the central focus of debate.[16] Unlike local budgets the federal budget can be financed by money creation.[17]

Russia conquered the hyperinflation which occurred in 1992 when a massive budget deficit was financed entirely by printing money. By 1997, inflation was at a relatively modest level. This was achieved by gradually reducing reliance on the printing press to finance persistently high, though generally declining, budget deficits. The federal budget deficit in 1995 was financed almost entirely by bond sales and external credits.[18] The federal budget deficit has remained stubbornly high, though, with problems on both the tax and spending sides (despite, as regards the latter, delays in the payment of state wages and pensions, a policy which is non-sustainable in the long run). The federal budget deficit, according to the IMF definition, was 7.9 per cent of GDP in 1996, 7.0 per cent in 1997 and 5 per cent in 1998.[19]

But heavy dependence on short-term borrowing ultimately proved to be unsustainable. This point has been stressed by a number of 'heavyweights' in the field:

The Russian authorities have been forced to attract increasing amounts of foreign funds to finance the deficit: by selling Treasury bills to foreigners and by borrowing from the international financial markets. This has resulted in an increase in the exposure of Russia to volatile short-term foreign capital.[20]

Russia's most immediate problem is that it has too large a short-term government debt in comparison with international reserves.[21]

The current crisis in Russia arose largely from a failure of the state - its inability to collect taxes, to enforce laws, to manage its employees and to pay them.[22]

At the root of Russia's macroeconomic problems have been persistently high federal budget deficits.[23]

The fundamental causes of the budget deficit were political: an inability to rein in government spending, weak tax discipline among politically influential firms and an excessive devolution of revenue to regional governments ... Politicians have been unwilling to draw sharp distinctions between public and private property or to impose hard budget constraints on large enterprises, both out of fear of the unemployment implications and to preserve rent-seeking opportunities for powerful vested interests.[24]

From 1995 the federal government financed much of its deficit by issuing short-term (less than one year) rouble-denominated Treasury bills (GKOs) and longer-dated coupon-bearing bonds (OFZs). Foreigners rushed into the high-yielding Russian debt market and, by the end of 1997, held an estimated 33 per cent of the total stock of GKOs and OFZs.[25]

Foreign investors in the GKO market were at first obliged, and many later chose, to hedge themselves against the risk of devaluation by buying dollar forward contracts with Russian banks. The hedge contracts increased the exposure of the Russian banking system to declines in the rouble.[26]

A word or two may be in order about the controversies surrounding exchange rate regimes and controls on capital flows. After mid-August 1998 the rate of exchange of the rouble against the US dollar quickly plunged from more than six to more than 20. There was a vociferous debate prior to 17 August 1998 about the policy of defending the rouble on the foreign exchange market.

According to one analysis:

a devaluation in Russia would be catastrophic ... The greatest achievement of the reformers has been to bring low inflation and financial stability. If they cannot even do that they will lose all credibility ... A devaluation would lead to an immediate increase in inflation and, even worse, to bank failures. And bank failures would lead to bankruptcies of enterprise. Unemployment would rise on a massive scale ... Without the Asian debâcle, there would be no crisis now in Russia. The G7 nations need to put together a stabilisation fund of at least US$10 billion which would be available for the Russian government.[27]

In another commentator's opinion:

> devaluation is not necessary because the rouble is not overvalued. Last year Russia had a huge trade surplus of US$20 billion and it has had similar trade surpluses for years ... Devaluation would undermine what little remaining confidence there was in the rouble and the exchange rate would drop by 80 to 90 per cent.[28]

However, Jeffrey Sachs, who was an economic adviser to the Russian government from December 1991 to January 1994, thinks the otherwise. He believes that exchange rates should generally float:

> It is neither worthwhile nor feasible to twist monetary policy to soothe panicky investors, especially at the cost of internal depression. The only real exception to floating rates comes at the start of stabilisation from extreme inflation, when exchange rate targeting is more efficient than monetary targeting.[29]

> Emerging market currencies should be allowed to float, since countries with pegged currencies too often run out of foreign reserves.[30]

My own view is that it makes no sense to use vital foreign exchange reserves to try to defend the exchange rate of a currency under attack in a deregulated world of massive and highly mobile private capital flows. There is an inherent weakness with a broadly fixed exchange rate regime, since private speculators are on an essentially 'one-way bet'. All that is at risk is relatively modest transactions costs, since a currency under heavy attack is not going to strengthen. Britain found this out to its cost when it was forced to leave the exchange rate mechanism of the European Monetary System in September 1992, and George Soros, for example, made a fortune. Thus much IMF aid to Russia was wasted in a futile defence of the currency. It would have been far better to have used what should have been generous Western aid to strengthen the legal and regulatory system and to encourage the development of civil society – the self-organisation of individuals in society.

Proponents of 'big bang'/ 'shock therapy' have always recommended rapid current account convertibility of currencies in transitional economies. But the Asian financial crisis has reinforced the view that capital account liberalisation ought to be a much slower and selective process. As Jeefrey Sachs said:

> Premature liberalisation of capital markets ... was one cause of the current crisis ... Developing countries should impose their own supervisory controls on short-term international borrowing by domestic financial institutions.[31]

Naturally, there is considerable debate about the merits of imposing controls on short-term capital flows. Critics argue, for example, that such controls are not very effective and that it would be better to concentrate on basic problems such as regulation.

## INSTITUTIONS AND TRANSITION

There is increasing recognition – in a general sense – that the institutional basis of a market economy takes a long time to put in place. Just think how long it has taken Western countries to develop appropriate political, legal and economic institutions and attitudes, including informal codes of behaviour such as 'gentlemen's agreements'. And yet even today massive financial scandals arise periodically. In transition economies there is a vital need for an efficient and honest legal system to enforce contracts and property rights. The vacuum that exists when the state is too weak to fulfil these vital functions is quickly filled by organised crime. What is particularly disturbing about countries like Russia is the common occurrence of links between the mafia and corrupt officials. Commentators state that:

> It is widely believed that a liberal economy is inconsistent with a strong government. But in fact a liberal economic systems *needs* (added italics) a strong government. It needs one because a liberal economy presumes laws and rules that are the same for everyone, and the only way to ensure such uniformity is through a strong government. One that tolerates no exceptions. One that cannot be bought. One that is capable of meeting out punishment[32]

> Key institutional foundations ... [include] an effective judicial and law enforcement system, the creation of a healthy commercial banking system, and a coherent policy for changing the structure of incentives so as to encourage entrepreneurship and fixed investment rather than rent-seeking and asset stripping.[33]

> Among the most damaging of the mistaken conclusions that were drawn early on in the transition process, both by Western advisers and by policy makers in Moscow, was that the Russian state remained too strong. The need to scale back inefficient spending, and to create room for private inefficient spending is a necessary task for which a strong public administration is required; but this is a quite different task from *restructuring* (added italics) the state so that it is strong enough and capable to perform the functions required to support a market economy.[34]

> Russian public administration is infamous for its lack of transparency and corruption.[35]

The European Bank for Reconstruction and Development (EBRD) has recently generalised the importance of institutional change in the next phase of transition by noting that:

Some aspects of a market economy can and have been created quickly in transition economies, in particular through market liberalisation and privatisation. However, developing the institutions and business practices required for a well-functioning market economy takes much longer.[36]

The imbalance has continued to widen between the earlier successes of privatisation and liberalisation and the more difficult structural and institutional challenges of the next phase of transition. These challenges include corporate governance and enterprise restructuring, financial sector reforms, infrastructure reform, and fiscal and social reforms ... The challenges of the next phase ... require a substantial and constructive role of the state at a time when its capacity is still underdeveloped and subject to capture by powerful economic interests.[37]

## GOOD GOVERNANCE AND PRIVATISATION

Compared with Western countries, privatisation in transition countries is of a different order of magnitude since the large industrial sectors were typically state-owned in the communist period. The potential for abuse is thus massive. Hence, there is a vital need for an honest, transparent and efficient government to control the privatisation process. The introduction of free and fair democratic elections is a necessary but not sufficient condition for ensuring this.

'Spontaneous' privatisation essentially means that managers and other members of the *nomenklatura* get their hands on state property at below market prices. Early forms of 'wild' spontaneous privatisation in Eastern Europe involved 'a more or less sophisticated theft from the state or society as a whole', such as obtaining shares or guaranteed jobs in the new companies.[38]

The first stage of Russian privatisation (1 October 1992–1 July 1994) was controversial because it clearly favoured 'insiders' (existing workers and managers), and was not conducive to restructuring.[39] But this was as nothing compared with other features. It was observed that:

When the economic reforms got underway in 1992 Russia's vast natural resources provided unparalleled opportunities for theft by officials. Oil, gas, diamond and metal ore deposits were nominally owned by the state and thus by nobody. They were ripe for stealing – or for "spontaneous privatisation" as Russians cynically call it... When natural resource enterprises were privatised the system was often skirted or compromised by ad hoc decrees and hidden arrangements. The biggest plums, the oil and gas enterprises, are worth tens of billions of dollars ... It is hard to know who owns Gazprom, the partly privatised natural gas giant, whose first chairman was Viktor Chernomyrdin, the prime minister.[40]

The government squandered tens of billions of dollars by transferring state-owned oil and gas companies to cronies at cut-rate prices.[41]

The oil and gas company executives were the prime advocates of low oil and gas prices. They bought oil at the domestic price on their own account and sold it abroad at the world market price ... The low domestic prices caused their companies losses, but that made shares in loss-making enterprises cheaper and the oil executives bought undervalued stock in the companies they managed for their illicit personal gains. This double fraud came to light in 1995 and it cannot survive for much longer.[42]

In the guise of privatisation, the population has been swindled of its national resources and industry by the people who are now manipulating its politics.[43]

Russian organised crime groups secured a massive transfer of state property because the privatisation occurred rapidly, on a huge scale, without legal safeguards, and without transparency ... The Russian mafia now controls more than 40 per cent of the total economy. In some sectors, such as consumer markets, real estate and banking, their role is even greater.[44]

The 'shares-for-loans' scheme in Russia was especially scandalous. This allowed certain Russian banks to assume management control of state shares in selected enterprises for use as collateral in return for loans. The low level of privatisation revenue raised by that time was a major consideration. Interest was to be paid and the loan was to be repaid within three years at the original value 'adjusted' for the intervening change in the rouble value of the European Currency Unit (ECU). If the lender and the state property committee agreed, the former could at any time sell the shares and keep the 'adjusted' value of the loan plus 30 per cent of the excess of the sale price over that value.[45] The government, however, did not repay the loans. The first round of mortgage auctions began on 17 November 1995 but the 'shares-for-loans' scheme was ended on 28 December 1995 owing to the vociferous criticism.

Abuses included the fact that banks which ran the auctions were allowed to bid! Observers noted that:

The 38 per cent stake in the largest nickel producer in the country, Norilsk Nikel, was won by Oneximbank (United Export Import Bank), Russia's largest private commercial bank and the bank responsible for organising the auction. One bidder who offered a much higher price was not allowed to take part in the auction[46]

There were few bidders owing to collusion among the potential buyers. The banks were allowed to impose tender conditions [such as future investment] on the buyer of the stake that would be difficult for any unaffiliated company to fulfil.[47]

Foreign investors were barred from bidding for the most desirable assets, and the same banks that were assigned by the government to organise the auctions ended up winning them, and usually at only a fraction over the minimum bid. Shares in some of Russia's largest oil conglomerates, including Lukoil and Yukos, were sold off for what Western analysts considered to be a fraction of their real value.[48]

Afraid that it had no political allies, the desperate Yeltsin administration decided to create some. The Kremlin's vehicle was the shares-for-loans privatisation scheme, which, over a few months in the autumn of 1995, transferred controlling stakes in some of Russia's most valuable companies to government insiders at a fraction of their potential worth. The programme provoked instant and outraged attacks at home and abroad. But it paid dividends at the ballot box on 3 July 1996, when Mr Yeltsin cruised to victory, aided by the vigorous organisational and material support of the small group of bankers he had made into billionaires.[49]

Mass (voucher) privatisation – in effect giving away assets to the population – has, like other schemes, advantages and disadvantages. Proponents point to 'fairness', speed and its relatively low potential for corruption. But opponents stress things like the lack of sales revenue and the difficulties of corporate governance (ensuring managers work to the benefit of owners). Czechoslovakia – the Czech Republic and Slovakia after the start of 1993 – adopted such a scheme.

The Czech Republic illustrates the dangers of lack of a proper system of corporate governance. In theory, investment funds – which accumulate sufficient shares to exercise control over companies – should provide a solution. But in the Czech Republic a peculiar situation arose where banks often controlled investment funds and the state retained large stakes in the largest banks. Such incestuous links between banks and enterprises led to all sorts of abuses, not least cronyism in the allocation of capital funds (as seen in some Asia countries). There is also the phenomenon of 'tunnelling', which involves investment fund managers defrauding shareholders by selling shares to 'dummy' companies – owned by managers themselves or their cronies – which then resell the shares at a profit. The general lack of regulation of capital markets in the heady, early post-communist days shows the importance of good governance even in a country which is a member of the North Atlantic Treaty Organisation (NATO) and a frontrunner for the European Union (EU).

Post-voucher privatisation in Slovakia under the Mečiar government (which lost office after the September 1998 general election) was mired in controversy:

> The privatisation process continues to be criticised for a lack of transparency. In June 1997 a 15 per cent stake in the petrochemical company Slovnaft was sold to the management for 20 per cent of the market price.[50]

> The style of privatisation has remained controversial. In February 1998 8 per cent of the shares of a large petrochemical company [Slovnaft] were sold for half the market price to a hitherto unknown company.[51]

> After abandoning the second wave of mass voucher privatisation in 1995, privatisation has continued via direct sales – usually to former management or domestic holding

companies. As foreigners have been virtually excluded from the privatisation process, they have played little role in the development of corporate governance.[52]

Critics argue that:

assets are sold only to those deemed loyal to Mr Mečiar's all-embracing Movement for a Democratic Slovakia (HZDS)".[53]

State factories are being sold to managers and HZDS cronies at knockdown rates – which can be paid in small long-term instalments. It will create a large stratum of politically loyal entrepreneurs – precisely what Mečiar wants. This could best be described as a corrupted plutocracy.[54]

The government continues its profoundly corrupt practice of 'privatising' state industry by giving it at concessionary prices exclusively to HZDS lackeys and supporters of the ruling parties.[55]

The Hungarian approach to privatisation has been to emphasise sales, especially to foreigners (partly as a result of its decision to repay its entire foreign debt). There has, of course, always been a debate about the pros and cons of direct foreign investment in any economy. But in an age of globalisation where financial panics can spread like prairie fires (through emerging markets at least), such investment must surely be given an additional plus. 'Infant-industry-like' arguments are sometimes used: for example, to shield domestic banks during their early years. But the financial crises since mid-1997 have painfully exposed the dangers (such as lack of competition and cronyism). Banks in transition economies surely need the sounder management and resources of reputable Western banks. Confidence is the name of the game these days and strong foreign backing is a way of overcoming one of the fundamental weaknesses which have laid low such a vitally important country as Russia.

## NOTES

1. Globalisation is the increasingly rapid integration of economies via such mechanisms as trade, capital flows, technology and information flows.
2. World Bank, *World Development Report: From Plan to Market* (New York 1996) p. 143.
3. Ibid, p. 9.
4. Ibid, p. 21.
5. *International Herald Tribune* (26 February 1999) p. 6.
6. *The Economist* (31 October 1998) p. 108.
7. *Financial Times* (29 August 1998) p. 10.
8. *Financial Times* (23 December 1998) p. 2.
9. *Financial Times* (18 April 1997) p. 2.

10. According to Boris Fyodorov, a former finance minister, in *Financial Times* (18 February 1999) p. 14.

11. *International Herald Tribune* (11 February 1999) p. 13.

12. Daniel Treisman, 'Russia's Taxing Problem', *Foreign Policy*, 112 (1998) p. 55.

13. David Hoffman, *International Herald Tribune* (27 February 1999) p. 1.

14. Anders Åslund, *International Herald Tribune* (29 April 1998) p. 10. Åslund was an early advisor to the Russian government.

15. Anders Åslund, *The World Today*, 54 (7 July 1998) pp. 185–6.

16. *Russian Economic Trends*, 3, 2 (1994) p. 9.

17. *Russian Economic Trends*, 3, 3 (1994) p. 10.

18. *Russian Economic Trends*, 4, 4 (1995) p. 5.

19. *Russian Economic Trends*, Monthly Update (20 January 1999) p. 24 and (10 February 1999) p. 10. The IMF definition holds that privatisation receipts and net sales of state gold reserves are counted as deficit financing. The European Union's Maastricht criterion as regards the budget deficit is a maximum of 3 per cent of GDP.

20. *United Nations Economic Commisison for Europe*, Economic Survey of Europe, 2 (Geneva 1998) pp. 24–5.

21. Anders Åslund, *Transition*, 9, 3 (1998) pp. 10–11.

22. *European Bank for Reconstruction and Development*, Transition Report (London 1998) p. iv.

23. Ibid., p. 14.

24. Ibid.

25. Ibid., p. 13.

26. Ibid., p. 14.

27. Richard Layard, *The Independent* (29 May 1998) p. 23.

28. Anders Åslund, *Transition*, pp. 10–11.

29. *The Economist* (12 September 1998) p. 24.

30. Jeffrey Sachs, *The Independent* (1 February 1999) p. 11.

31. Jeffrey Sachs, *The Economist*, (12 September 1998) p. 24.

32. According to Pyotr Aven, president of Alphabank and former minister of foreign economic relations in Russia, *Current Digest of the Post-Soviet Press*, 51.7 (1999) p. 5.

33. United Nations Economic Commission for Europe, Europe *Economic Survey of 1998* (New York 1998) p. 10.

34. Ibid., p. 9.

35. Ibid., p. 34.

36. European Bank for Reconstruction and Development, *Transition Report* (London 1998) p. iv.

37. Ibid., pp. vi–vii.

38. United Nations Economic Commission for Europe, *Economic Survey of Europe in 1991–92* (New York 1992) p. 231.

39. 'Insider' privatisation is a more accurate description than 'voucher' privatisation.

40. Jeffrey Sachs, *International Herald Tribune* (6 December 1995) p. 10.

41. Jeffrey Sachs, *International Herald Tribune* (5 June 1998) p. 8.

42. Anders Åslund, *Business Central Europe*, The Annual (1995) p. 15.

43. William Pfaff, *International Herald Tribune* (22 April 1998) p. 9.

44. Louise Shelley, *Transition*, 8,1 (February 1997) p. 7.

45. *Russian Economic Trends*, Monthly Update (19 September 1995) p. 11.
46. *Russian Economic Trends*, 4, 3 (1995) pp. 93–4 and 100–2.
47. *Russian Economic Trends*, 1, 3 (1997) p. 151.
48. Alessandra Stanley, *International Herald Tribune* (29 January 1996) p. 11.
49. Chrystia Freeland, *Financial Times*, Survey (9 April 1997) p. i.
50. *European Bank for Reconstruction and Development*, Transition Report (London 1997) p. 198.
51. European Bank for Reconstruction and Development, *Transition Report Update* (London 1998) p. 41.
52. European Bank for Reconstruction and Development, *Transition Report* (London 1998) pp. 188–9.
53. *Financial Times*, survey (20 December 1995) p. iv.
54. *Eastern European Newsletter* 10, 8 (1996) pp. 5–6.
55. *Eastern European Newsletter* 11, 24 (1997) p. 2.

# 3. Recovery and Growth in Transition Economies, 1990–97: A Stylised Regression Analysis

**Oleh Havrylyshyn, Ivailo Izvorski and Ron van Rooden**[1]

## INTRODUCTION

The process of transition is a unique historical event, and analysing it is not easy since this is a complex, multidimensional process encompassing not only economic changes but also profound changes in political and social relations. If one were to seek a simplifying core theme, perhaps the common thread tying together the different country experiences of transition is the objective of improved economic well-being of the population.

It has been nearly a decade since the transition began – first in Central Europe in 1989–90, then further East – and an initial glance at statistics would suggest growth is becoming widespread (Table 3.1), with only two countries, Ukraine and Turkmenistan, still experiencing a continued decline through 1997. Three others, Albania, Bulgaria and Romania, experienced a (perhaps) premature burst of growth in the mid-1990s suffering a reversal in 1996–97. But even for the others, the growth rates with a few exceptions (Estonia, Georgia, Poland) are not extraordinarily high by historical standards, certainly not high enough to allow these countries to catch up quickly even to low-income Western European countries.[2]

In 1997, While the average growth rate for the 20 growing countries was 4.8 per cent, in seven countries the rate was below 3 per cent. Further, the recovery is very recent: only 11 countries have entered a period of thus far sustained growth of three or more years, and only in 1995 did half of the 25 transition countries reach positive growth. It is also still fragile, as demonstrated by the three cases of reversal. It is none the less instructive to consider what factors are associated with recovery or lack of it in transition economies, in order to draw some conclusions for appropriate policies to promote sustained growth.

*Table 3.1 Growth of GDP in transition economies, percentage change from previous year (1990–1997)*

|  | 1990 | 1991 | 1992 | 1993 | 1994 | 1995 | 1996 | 1997 |
|---|---|---|---|---|---|---|---|---|
| *Central and Eastern Europe* | | | | | | | | |
| Albania | −10.0 | −28.0 | −7.2 | 9.6 | 9.4 | 8.9 | 9.1 | −7.0 |
| Bulgaria | −9.1 | −11.7 | −7.3 | −1.5 | 1.8 | 2.9 | −10.1 | −6.9 |
| Croatia | −7.1 | −21.1 | −11.7 | −8.0 | 5.9 | 6.8 | 6.0 | 6.5 |
| Czech R. | −1.2 | −14.3 | −3.3 | 0.6 | 2.7 | 6.4 | 3.9 | 1.0 |
| Macedonia | −10.2 | −12.1 | −8.0 | −9.1 | −1.8 | −1.2 | 0.8 | 1.5 |
| Hungary | −3.5 | −11.9 | −3.1 | −0.6 | 2.9 | 1.5 | 1.3 | 4.4 |
| Poland | −11.6 | −7.0 | 2.6 | 3.8 | 5.2 | 7.0 | 6.1 | 6.9 |
| Romania | −5.6 | −12.9 | −8.8 | 1.5 | 3.9 | 7.1 | 3.9 | −6.6 |
| Slovak R. | −2.5 | −14.6 | −6.5 | −3.7 | 4.9 | 6.9 | 6.6 | 6.5 |
| Slovenia | −8.1 | −8.9 | −5.5 | 2.8 | 5.3 | 4.1 | 3.1 | 3.7 |
| *Average* | −7.0 | −14.7 | −5.9 | -0.4 | 4.1 | 5.2 | 3.3 | 1.0 |
| *Baltic States* | | | | | | | | |
| Estonia | −8.1 | −7.9 | −21.6 | −8.2 | −1.8 | 4.3 | 4.0 | 10.8 |
| Latvia | 2.9 | −10.4 | −35.2 | −16.1 | 2.1 | 0.3 | 3.3 | 6.5 |
| Lithuania | −5.0 | −13.4 | −21.3 | −16.2 | −9.8 | 3.3 | 4.7 | 5.7 |
| *Average* | −3.4 | −10.6 | −26.0 | −13.3 | −3.4 | 2.8 | 4.0 | 7.9 |
| *Commonwealth of Independent States* | | | | | | | | |
| Armenia | −7.4 | −17.1 | −52.3 | −14.8 | 5.4 | 6.9 | 5.8 | 3.3 |
| Azerbaijan | −11.7 | −0.7 | −22.1 | −23.1 | −18.1 | −11.0 | 1.3 | 5.7 |
| Belarus | −3.0 | −1.2 | −9.6 | −7.6 | −12.6 | −10.4 | 2.8 | 10.4 |
| Georgia | −12.4 | −13.8 | −44.8 | −25.4 | −11.4 | 2.4 | 10.5 | 11.0 |
| Kazakhstan | −0.4 | −13.0 | −5.3 | −9.2 | −12.6 | −8.2 | 0.5 | 2.0 |
| Kyrgyz R. | 3.2 | −5.0 | −13.9 | −15.5 | −20.1 | −5.4 | 7.1 | 6.5 |
| Moldova | −2.4 | −17.5 | −29.7 | −1.2 | −31.2 | −1.4 | −7.8 | 1.3 |
| Russia | −4.0 | −5.0 | −14.5 | −8.7 | −12.6 | −4.0 | −2.8 | 0.4 |
| Tajikistan | −1.6 | −7.1 | −29.0 | −11.0 | −18.9 | −12.5 | −4.4 | 2.2 |
| Turkmenistan | −2.0 | −4.7 | −5.3 | −10.2 | −19.0 | −8.2 | −7.7 | −25.0 |
| Ukraine | −3.4 | −11.9 | −17.0 | −14.2 | −22.9 | −12.2 | −10.0 | −3.2 |
| Uzbekistan | 1.6 | −0.5 | −11.0 | −2.3 | −4.2 | −0.9 | 1.6 | 2.1 |
| *Average* | −3.3 | −8.1 | −21.2 | −11.4 | −15.4 | −5.8 | −0.4 | 1.3 |

*Source:* National Authorities; IMF staff estimates.

The early years of transition have been characterised by a sharp contraction in output following the disruption of traditional trade and financial links, and the abandonment of old central plan lines of production. This was generally followed by attempts to maintain production and employment at previous levels by running large fiscal and quasi-fiscal deficits, resulting in high rates of inflation – particularly after countries had introduced their own currencies – and further collapses in output. After this common experience, most transition countries engaged in comprehensive stabilisation and reform programmes, often supported by the International Monetary Fund (IMF). Although countries that implemented such programmes generally succeeded in bringing down inflation to low levels, the success in achieving sustained growth has been more varied. Those that started stabilisation earlier experienced earlier recovery, but the timing, strength and sustainability of growth also depended on progress in structural reforms.

In Table 3.2 it is seen that for Central and Eastern European countries and the Baltic states, inflation reached its peak in 1992 and reasonably low rates of inflation were established by 1994, the same year in which growth resumed.[3] In the countries of the Commonwealth of Independent States (CIS) this process took place on average two years later, with growth resuming only in 1996/97.[4]

This second table also shows that countries in Central and Eastern Europe started earlier in implementing structural reforms and on average have made considerably more progress, as indicated by the higher level of the reform index.[5] Progress on structural reforms in CIS countries has been much slower, with the median value of the reform index in 1997 still only at the 1991 level of Central and Eastern European countries. Although this has not prevented the resumption of growth on average two to three years after the start of the disinflation process, the economic rebound in the CIS countries has been weaker. As can be seen in Table 3.1, the group average for the CIS became positive only in 1997, at 1.3 per cent, whereas in the Baltic states, it had been positive for three years (averaging 4.9 per cent) and in Central and Eastern Europe for four years (averaging 2.6 per cent). While slower progress in reforms is one possible explanation, another is less-favourable initial conditions in CIS countries compared with Central and Eastern European countries.

Although positive growth of gross domestic product (GDP) in transition is a very recent phenomenon, a large number of studies have used econometric analysis to analyse the determinants of growth. The present study does not purport to improve upon the methodology of those studies, and differs from them only in four ways. First, the data available cover the period through 1997 and therefore provide a much longer period of positive growth observations. Most earlier studies include data only through 1995 or at best 1996.[6] Second, the period covered is long enough to allow separate econometric analysis of two subperiods, defined broadly as the decline or negative growth period (1990–93) and the recovery or positive growth period (1994–97).

This permits a test of the hypothesis that explanations for decline are different from explanations of growth. Third, we address more explicitly than other studies the trade-off between unfavourable initial conditions and favourable policies. Fourth, the econometric model specification here is a compact, 'stylised facts', compromise between models using very simple regressions relating growth and a single measure of reform progress[7] and much more complex specifications including a large number of variables, time-lag effects, and dynamic inter-relations.[8] The former are clearly underspecified, while the latter are not always easy to interpret because of the complex lags and inter-relationships, and the unmeasurable country-specific fixed effects estimates.

The rest of the chapter is organised as follows. The next section briefly reviews a selected set of writings on growth in general and in transition countries specifically. Subsequently, the model used and data sources are specified, after which the results of the regression analysis are described. The final section presents the key conclusions and policy implications.

*Table 3.2 Summary statistics of growth, inflation and structural reforms in transition economies (1990–1997)*[*]

| | 1990 | 1991 | 1992 | 1993 | 1994 | 1995 | 1996 | 1997 |
|---|---|---|---|---|---|---|---|---|
| *Growth* | | | | | | | | |
| All countries | | | | | | | | |
| Average | −4.7 | −10.9 | −15.7 | −7.5 | −5.9 | −0.3 | 1.6 | 2.0 |
| Median | −4.0 | −11.9 | −11.0 | −8,0 | −1.8 | 1.5 | 3.1 | 3.3 |
| Highest | 3.2 | −0.5 | 2.6 | 9.6 | 9.4 | 8.9 | 10.5 | 11.0 |
| Lowest | -12.4 | −28.0 | −52.3 | −25.4 | −31.2 | −12.5 | −10.1 | −25.0 |
| | | | | | | | | |
| Central and Eastern Europe | | | | | | | | |
| Average | −6.1 | −13.4 | −10.5 | −3.5 | 2.4 | 4.5 | 3.3 | 2.5 |
| Median | −7.1 | −12.1 | −7.3 | −1.5 | 2.9 | 4.3 | 3.9 | 4.4 |
| Highest | 2.9 | −7.0 | 2.6 | 9.6 | 9.4 | 8.9 | 9.1 | 10.8 |
| Lowest | −11.6 | −28.0 | −35.2 | −16.2 | −9.8 | −1.2 | −10.1 | −7.0 |
| | | | | | | | | |
| Commonwealth of Independent States | | | | | | | | |
| Average | −3.3 | −8.1 | −21.2 | 11.4 | −15.4 | −5.8 | −0.4 | 1.3 |
| Median | −2.7 | −6.1 | −15.8 | 10.6 | −15.4 | −6.8 | 0.9 | 2.1 |
| Highest | 3.2 | −0.5 | −5.3 | −1.2 | 5.4 | 6.9 | 10.5 | 11.0 |
| Lowest | −12.4 | −17.5 | −52.3 | −25.4 | −31.2 | −12.5 | −10.0 | −25.0 |
| | | | | | | | | |
| *Inflation* | | | | | | | | |
| All countries | | | | | | | | |
| Average | 63.4 | 115.5 | 741.8 | 1071.0 | 1312.0 | 178.1 | 87.0 | 72.6 |
| Median | 8.4 | 98.0 | 853.8 | 543.2 | 136.7 | 39.5 | 23.5 | 14.7 |
| Highest | 585.8 | 333.5 | 1925.2 | 4735.0 | 15607. | 1005.0 | 992.0 | 1082.2 |
| Lowest | 3.0 | 34.8 | 10.1 | 20.8 | 10.2 | 2.0 | 2.3 | 2.9 |
| | | | | | | | | |
| Central and Eastern Europe | | | | | | | | |
| Average | 117.4 | 134.8 | 495.7 | 224.7 | 56.3 | 23.2 | 24.2 | 11.5 |
| Median | 22.0 | 122.2 | 210.4 | 85.1 | 35.9 | 25.1 | 18.8 | 9.1 |
| Highest | 585.8 | 333.5 | 1925.2 | 1515.6 | 136.7 | 62.1 | 123.0 | 1082.2 |
| Lowest | 5.1 | 34.8 | 10.1 | 20.8 | 10.2 | 2.0 | 2.3 | 2.9 |
| | | | | | | | | |
| Commonwealth of Independent States | | | | | | | | |
| Average | 4.9 | 93.7 | 1008.5 | 1988. | 2672.0 | 346.0 | 155.1 | 37.7 |
| Median | 4.2 | 93.4 | 940.8 | 1426. | 1616.4 | 247.3 | 43.6 | 16.6 |
| Highest | 10.3 | 111.6 | 1515.7 | 4735. | 15607. | 1005.3 | 992.0 | 98.0 |
| Lowest | 3.0 | 78.5 | 492.9 | 534.2 | 228.7 | 30.2 | 18.7 | 3.9 |

|  | 1990 | 1991 | 1992 | 1993 | 1994 | 1995 | 1996 | 1997 |
|---|---|---|---|---|---|---|---|---|
| *Reform Index* | | | | | | | | |
| All countries | | | | | | | | |
| Average | 0.19 | 0.33 | 0.51 | 0.57 | 0.61 | 0.60 | 0.62 | 0.64 |
| Median | 0.04 | 0.24 | 0.49 | 0.60 | 0.67 | 0.60 | 0.62 | 0.63 |
| Highest | 0.68 | 0.79 | 0.86 | 0.90 | 0.88 | 0.81 | 0.81 | 0.85 |
| Lowest | 0.00 | 0.04 | 0.13 | 0.13 | 0.29 | 0.26 | 0.26 | 0.35 |
| | | | | | | | | |
| Central and Eastern Europe | | | | | | | | |
| Average | 0.33 | 0.55 | 0.71 | 0.77 | 0.76 | 0.69 | 0.71 | 0.73 |
| Median | 0.20 | 0.62 | 0.72 | 0.79 | 0.79 | 0.68 | 0.71 | 0.73 |
| Highest | 0.68 | 0.79 | 0.86 | 0.90 | 0.88 | 0.81 | 0.81 | 0.85 |
| Lowest | 0.00 | 0.24 | 0.45 | 0.58 | 0.63 | 0.56 | 0.56 | 0.61 |
| | | | | | | | | |
| Commonwealth of Independent States | | | | | | | | |
| Average | 0.04 | 0.10 | 0.29 | 0.36 | 0.45 | 0.50 | 0.53 | 0.54 |
| Median | 0.04 | 0.10 | 0.29 | 0.34 | 0.42 | 0.50 | 0.56 | 0.58 |
| Highest | 0.04 | 0.22 | 0.49 | 0.60 | 0.71 | 0.68 | 0.68 | 0.70 |
| Lowest | 0.04 | 0.04 | 0.13 | 0.13 | 0.29 | 0.26 | 0.26 | 0.35 |

*Note:*     * The 1997 average for inflation excludes Bulgaria and Romania, where inflation reached very high levels after the growth reversal.

*Sources:* National authorities, Martha de Melo, Cevdet Denizer and Alan Gelb, 'From Plan to Market: Patterns of Transition', Policy Research Department, Transition Economic Division, The World Bank (Washington DC 1996); European Bank for Reconstruction and Development, Transition Report (London various years); IMF staff estimates.

# REVIEW OF TRANSITION LITERATURE

## General Growth Theory

A revival of interest in economic growth in the mid-1980s led to the development of a new wave of models which established a synthesis now known as *endogenous growth theory*. The first element of this synthesis is the earlier prevailing doctrine on economic growth – the neoclassical models of Solow–Swan and Cass–Koopmans from the 1950s to the 1960s – which attributed growth to the expansion of capital and labour, augmented by exogenous technological progress. Simple factor input and factor productivity calculations of the sources of growth are based on this paradigm and continue to be used widely. The second element is the set of models developed in the mid-1980s.[9] While retaining the role of factor inputs, these models added an explanation of technical progress based on increasing returns, research and development (R&D) and imperfect competition, human capital, and – an important addition – government policies. The role of policies was initially focused narrowly on economic measures such as macroeconomic stability, openness of the economy and degree of distortion in key price signals. A third element – property rights policies – has been added, borrowing from political economy models. Olson, in particular, summarised well the role of policy areas such as property rights, rule of law, institutions and corruption.[10] He argues that both of the preceding models assume, incorrectly, that countries (and policymakers) make the most efficient use of resource inputs and available technology; instead, he posited that many countries are poor simply because they waste a lot of resources. On the basis of earlier work on the political economy of interest groups, he then added that the waste was greatest where the institutional basis of property rights and rule of law was least well developed or poorly observed in practice; a negative association between growth and corruption readily follows from this.

The past decade has seen numerous empirical studies based on this synthesised model seeking to explain the observed wide differences in growth patterns across countries and over time, including as determinants: *factor inputs* (investment, human capital); *government policies* (monetary and fiscal policy, price distortions); and *indicators of property rights security* (tax burden and its fairness, corruption, transparency, political stability and so on). It is useful to review briefly the key conclusions from this recent literature.[11]

First, initial conditions are important in explaining inter-country differences in growth. In particular, most studies have found that per capita growth is inversely related to the initial level of output, and, once other factors are accounted for, poor countries tend to grow faster than rich ones. Further, greater availability of resources does not necessarily ensure growth, while unfavourable geographic circumstances (tropical climate, a land-locked position) can hinder it. Second, good economic policy (macroeconomic stability and non-distortive interventions) has a strong effect on growth. Thus, reducing inflation not only to levels below 30 to 40 per cent as thought earlier but even lower seems to be a necessary condition for achieving sustained growth.[12] Policies that lower or distort the rate of return on private capital, such as high taxes, exchange or import controls and price regulations are highly likely to reduce the growth performance of a country. Third, the legal, political and institutional framework also matters a great deal. Most recent empirical studies make some attempt to capture the latter and usually find that growth is higher with better institutional quality, political stability, government credibility and similar indicators of a market-friendly environment.

**Applicability to Transition Economies**

In this section we first consider what kind of core framework of transition is available as a basis for analysing growth; second, we use this to infer which conclusions from general growth literature apply to the process of transition; and third, we review briefly previous empirical studies of growth in transition economies.

It is still frequently said that there is no theory to guide the practical process of transition, only theories of capitalism and socialism. This may still be true in the sense that no new consensus paradigm has emerged from the vast literature on transition, but it is not at all clear how much a unified, cohesive theory is needed to understand the main developments. Besides, to the extent that it is useful to have a compact rather than complex analytical framework, it is not that difficult to cobble together from a selected few of the key writings a workable 'model' of transition or transformation. Kornai, in describing the special circumstances of the 'transformational' recession compared with a market economy recession, highlights two key changes that are needed: forcing a move from a sellers' to a buyers' market (via price liberalisation) and enforcing a hard budget constraint (via privatisation and elimination of various government support mechanisms such as budget subsidies, directed low cost credits, and tax exemptions).[13] These provide the two principal incentives for profit-maximising market behaviour of all economic agents. Blanchard defines the core process of actual change as comprising two elements: reallocation of resources from old to new activities (via closures and bankruptcies combined with the establishment of new enterprises); and restructuring within surviving firms (via labour rationalisation, product line change and new investment).[14] These can be thought of as the dynamic movements resulting from the establishment of the new incentives and are very reminiscent of the Schumpeterian concept of 'creative destruction' by entrepreneurial activity, though with much greater and faster impact than Schumpeter's model envisaged.[15]

The policy actions needed to put in place Kornai's new incentives are described in many works, and are well exemplified by an early study of Fischer and Gelb, who outline the key measures of reform:[16]

- macroeconomic stabilisation; price and market liberalisation;
- liberalisation of the exchange and trade system;
- privatisation of state-owned firms;
- establishing a competitive environment with easy market entry and exit;
- redefining the role of the state as the provider of macro stability, a stable legal framework, enforceable property rights, and occasionally as a corrector of market imperfections.

From such a core concept of transformation there follow some implications for growth which differentiate the transition economies from market economies and which provide the basis for empirical analysis of determinants of recovery in transition.

First, output will necessarily decline initially under the new buyer's market and hard budget constraints, since unsaleable goods accumulate and signal the need for cutbacks in production. Further elimination of the wastage found under the old regime necessarily precedes the creation of the new, adding to the production cuts. Second, growth of the new will not occur until the new incentives are in place and made credible. Thus the sooner reforms achieve a hard budget and liberal price environment, the sooner reallocation and the restructuring of the old and the creation of new production can begin. Third, the proximate mechanisms in the early recovery period are most probably a variety of efficiency improvements rather than expansion of factor inputs, either investment or labour. There is a consensus in the general growth literature that investment is a major engine of growth in the medium to long term; but, in transition economies with substantial inherited inefficiencies as well as underutilised capacity, the short-run role of new investment is likely to be relatively less important, at least for the initial recovery.[17] Some suggestive evidence comes from trends in the investment to GDP ratio. Of 17 countries with so far sustained growth and adequate data on investment, the most common pattern for the investment to GDP ratio is a decline from the central plan period levels of 30 per cent and more to near 20 per cent or even lower. Further, for the 17 countries an upturn in the ratio of investment to output preceded the recovery in only three cases, while it coincided with the beginning of recovery in five countries and actually lagged the upturn in output in nine cases. It is therefore not surprising that the recent empirical studies on growth during transition, while borrowing strongly from the new growth theory, ignore the long-term factors such as investment, and focus on efficiency-improving factors such as macro policies, structural reforms and the property rights climate. This chapter continues in that spirit.

We conclude this section with a brief summary of earlier empirical studies. The first and probably least controversial conclusion is that stabilisation is a necessary (but not sufficient) condition for recovery of output.[18] The apparent exceptions of Bulgaria and Romania fell into line when their growth and then stabilisation reversed in 1997, but two exceptions exist at present – Belarus and Uzbekistan – and we discuss later their similarity to the reversal cases.

Second, but somewhat more controversial, emphasis was also put on the additional, necessary conditions to promote growth, that is, liberalisation and structural reforms. Whether the framework was a simple one relating only growth and some index of structural reforms,[19] or a more complex one reflecting also the effects of stabilisation, initial conditions, conflicts, and so on[20] the conclusion was firm: more reforms are associated with better growth performance. The results are not without exceptions, Belarus and Uzbekistan today being the key ones, and Bulgaria and Romania earlier. Taube and Zettelmeyer show for Uzbekistan that structural and macroeconomic policies alone cannot explain the better than average performance and find that initial conditions, in particular the low degree of industrialisation and cotton export potential, helped cushion the decline and perhaps promote an earlier recovery.[21] Some authors point to a dichotomy in the literature concerning the pace of reforms, while theoretical work on transition has often shown that a gradual pace might lead to less early decline of output: empirical studies generally conclude that fast and early reforms result in early and strong recovery.[22]

A third set of conclusions relates to initial conditions (for example, high degree of industrialisation) and other factors specific to countries such as wars. It is generally agreed that these do have an effect that is country specific, though different studies attribute a different magnitude of importance. De Melo et al. in a study which groups many different initial conditions, find a substantial impact; Åslund et al. also argue the more inward-looking and generally overindustrialised economies in the former Union of Soviet Socialist Republics (USSR) faced a bigger hurdle than did Central Europe.[23] Berg et al. conclude that achievement of stabilisation and progress in structural reforms (that is, policies) explain most of the difference between, for example, the better growth performance of Central and Eastern Europe and the poorer performance of the CIS.[24] A different way of looking at this will be addressed in the present chapter: how much of a trade-off is there between better policies and less-favourable initial conditions?[25]

A fourth set of conclusions relates to the market-enhancing nature of institutions such as the rule of law, corruption climate, the tax burden and its fairness. These factors are even less easily measured than the degree of liberalisation, hence not surprisingly the statistic used varies a great deal among studies. Despite this, many studies suggest that growth is higher where market-enhancing institutions are strongest.[26]

## MODEL SPECIFICATION

To determine the relative importance of the factors described above in explaining variations in countries' economic performance, we have conducted a simplified econometric analysis of economic growth in transition economies. At the start it is useful to remember the limitations of any econometric analysis. Growth is a complex process having many possible determinants, and theory does not provide a clear consensus on the 'correct' model specification. Harberger usefully points out that, at heart, growth is the sum of a 'thousand and one' individual initiatives by entrepreneurs and managers to make improvements in products and production processes, and therefore (he contends) regression analysis does not 'explain' growth, but can at best illustrate its nature by organising stylised facts.[27] The present chapter takes such an approach and opts for a limited specification, which focuses on a few of the key factors that can be thought of as the stylised facts of growth in transition economies.

A second important limitation is posed by the considerable data caveats that apply, particularly regarding output data, which are likely to be seriously biased for both conceptual and measurement reasons. At the conceptual level, the prices at which output was valued before the transition process began were out of line, while the calculation of volume changes suffers from the use of often arbitrary 'comparative' prices. At the measurement level, coverage is poor because the statistical systems that were designed to collect information from state-owned enterprises are likely to miss a large part of the emerging private sector. In addition, while state-owned enterprises used to have an incentive to over-report their production, both state-owned and private enterprises now have an incentive to under-report in order to avoid taxation or regulations. We do not attempt here to take account of the well-known problem of the 'unofficial economy'.[28]

All of the estimated equations have the growth rate of real gross domestic product (*GR*) as the dependent variable. As independent variables we include variables that represent those factors believed to be important in explaining economic performance as discussed above. Thus, to represent economic policies we include the natural logarithm of inflation (*LNP*) representing macroeconomic policies; a structural reform index (*RI*) representing the level of structural reforms achieved; and the size of the government, measured by general government expenditures as a percentage of GDP (*EXP*), representing factors such as crowding-out, distortions through high taxation, and large bureaucracies. To represent initial conditions we use two "clusters" of initial conditions, the first capturing macroeconomic distortions and unfamiliarity with market processes (*INCOND1*)[29] and the second the level of socialist development and its associated distortions (*INCOND2*).[30] For a simpler, stylised interpretation of initial conditions, we also used 1989 levels of per capita income (*INC*), the degree of industrialisation in 1990 (*ID*), and the deviation from the average degree of industrialisation in 1990 (*IDDEV*) separately. The data commonly used in growth studies to represent evolution of market-enhancing institutions – corruption indices, rule of law, country risk values – are available only for a handful of transition countries in this period. We do, however, use an indicator for the extensiveness and effectiveness of the legal framework (*LEG*) for which data are available for the 1995–97 period.

Data on growth and inflation (consumer price index, year-on-year change) are official data provided by the authorities, while data for the reform index were taken from de Melo et al. for the years 1990–93, then linked through 1997 to the transition indicators in the EBRD Transition Reports.[31] Data on government expenditures are official data and Fund staff estimates. Variables representing initial conditions were taken from de Melo et al..[32]

Our estimated specifications were of the following general forms, which we refer to as stylised regressions:

$$GR_{i,t} = a_i + b_0LNP_{i,t} + c_0RI_{i,t} + c_1RI_{i,t-1} + c_2RI_{i,t-2} + d_0EXP_{i,t} + \varepsilon_{i,t} \qquad (3.1)$$

and:

$$GR_{i,t} = a_0 + b_0LNP_{i,t} + c_0RI_{i,t} + c_1RI_{i,t-1} + c_2RI_{i,t-2} + d_0EXP_{i,t} + e_0INCOND1_i + e_1INCOND2_i + \varepsilon_{i,t} \qquad (3.2)$$

These equations were estimated with panel data for the 25 transition economies for the years 1990–97 (which provides up to 200 observations, depending on data availability of individual variables), with $i$ and $t$ indexing the country and the time period.

In general, one would expect higher inflation to have a negative impact on economic growth, that is, that $b_0 < 0$. Greater degrees of structural reforms would be expected to have a positive overall effect on growth. However, both theory and earlier empirical studies suggest that reforms may have at first a negative effect on growth – Schumpeter's 'destruction' – but, after a lag, the effect becomes positive, increasing in proportion to the accumulated stock of reforms – Schumpeter's 'creation'. Thus, in specifications including the contemporaneous value of the reform index, as well as two lagged values, we then would expect that $c_0 < 0$, and $c_1$ and $c_2 > 0$, and $c_1 + c_2 > |c_0|$ so that reforms have an overall positive effect on growth over time.

The expected effect of government size is less clear-cut. While it is well known that the share of government spending is positively associated with the level of development, this correlation, known as Wagner's Law, is not the same as saying more government gives higher growth. One could also expect a negative impact of 'large government' on growth because of high tax rates, crowding-out and restrictive red tape. Indeed, the growth literature demonstrates on a cross-section of countries that, for a given initial level of per capita GDP, lower government consumption is associated with higher long-run growth rates.[33] For transition countries it has sometimes been argued that after an initial stabilisation, looser fiscal policy and increased government spending may boost growth in the short run through an aggregate demand stimulus. But, as Kornai noted, the latter, Keynesian effects, would be relevant only after a hard budget environment is solidly in place; as long as the 'socialist' bias of government expenditures toward less productive sectors continues, the effect is likely to be negative. Thus on balance we expect that $d_0 < 0$.[34]

The first cluster of initial conditions from the de Melo et al. study represents macroeconomic distortions at the start of transition; the greater such distortions, the less growth (thus $e_0 < 0$).[35] Similarly for the second cluster representing structural distortions, greater distortions result in less growth ($e_1 < 0$). The simpler alternative variables for initial conditions are also expected to be negatively correlated with growth. *INC*, the 1989 level of per capita income, is included to test the common hypothesis in growth theory that incomes converge, that is, low income countries grow faster. *ID*, the share of industry in GDP, is considered to be a proxy for degree of distortions inherited from the socialist period, that is, higher values impede or slow recovery.

## EMPIRICAL RESULTS

### Explanatory Power of the Regression Model

Tables 3.3 and 3.4 present the econometric results. Table 3.3 shows panel estimates for the entire sample period, 1990–97, while the two panels of Table 3.4 provide estimates for the two subperiods, 1990–93 and 1994–97. Two equations representing the main results (3.A4 and 3.A10) are also reported below:

$$GR_{i,t} = -1.98 * LNP_{i,t} - 8.16 * RI_{i,t} + 16.94 * RI_{i,t-1} + 11.08 * RI_{i,t-2}$$

$$(-10.44) \quad (-1.61) \quad (2.94) \quad (2.40)$$

$$-0.11 * EXP_{i,t} - 2.55 * INCOND2 \qquad (3.A4)$$

$$(-3.00) \qquad (-4.23)$$

$$R^2 \text{ adj.} = 0.76$$

$$GR_{i,t} = -1.10 * LNP_{i,t} - 0.62 * LNP_{i,t-1} - 8.76 * RI_{i,t} + 20.31 * RI_{i,t-1}$$

$$(-4.89) \quad (-2.68) \quad (-2.20) \quad (4.36)$$

$$+ 7.04 * RI_{i,t-2} - 0.15 * EXP_{i,t} - 0.08 * IDDEV \qquad (3.A10)$$

$$(3.39) \qquad (-5.50) \qquad (-2.41)$$

$$R^2 \text{ adj.} = 0.77$$

Table 3.3  *Growth determinants: panel estimates for policy variables and initial conditions (1990–1997)**

| | LNP | LNP-1 | RI | RI-1 | RI-2 | EXP | INC | ID | IDDEV | FSU DUM | $R^2$ Adj. |
|---|---|---|---|---|---|---|---|---|---|---|---|
| 3.A1 | -2.57 | | 11.34 | | | | | | | | 0.76 |
| | 17.54 | | 10.67 | | | | | | | | |
| 3.A2 | -2.07 | | 14.80 | 14.74 | 11.96 | | | | | | 0.54 |
| | 11.92 | | -2.85 | 2.37 | 4.19 | | | | | | |
| 3.A3 | -2.32 | | 10.77 | 15.80 | 10.60 | | | | | | 0.72 |
| | 11.28 | | -2.09 | 2.74 | 4.58 | | | | | | |
| 3.A4 | -1.98 | | -8.16 | 16.94 | 11.08 | -0.11 | | | | | 0.75 |
| | 10.44 | | -1.60 | 2.94 | 2.40 | -3.00 | | | | | |
| 3.A5 | -1.96 | | -8.11 | 16.88 | 11.07 | -0.11 | | | | -0.15 | 0.76 |
| | -8.64 | | -1.60 | 2.92 | 4.58 | -2.99 | | | | -0.17 | |
| 3.A6 | -1.75 | | -6.76 | 15.53 | 12.51 | -0.10 | 0.001 | | | | 0.76 |
| | -9.14 | | -1.26 | 2.59 | 4.91 | -2.88 | -2.920 | | | | |
| 3.A7 | | | 21.20 | 26.96 | 11.80 | -0.28 | | | | | 0.66 |
| | | | -3.82 | 4.07 | 3.85 | -8.53 | | | | | |
| 3.A8 | | | 16.89 | 27.15 | 11.85 | -0.23 | | | | | 0.68 |
| | | | -2.71 | 4.11 | 3.99 | -6.29 | | | | | |
| 3.A9 | | | 16.11 | 31.70 | 12.94 | -0.22 | 0.001 | -0.11 | | -7.64 | 0.63 |
| | | | -2.76 | 4.82 | 3.91 | -6.15 | -2.590 | -3.29 | | -1.94 | |
| 3.A10 | -1.10 | -0.62 | -8.76 | 20.31 | 7.04 | -0.15 | | | -0.08 | | 0.77 |
| | -4.98 | -2.68 | -2.20 | 4.36 | 3.39 | -5.50 | | | -2.41 | | |

*Notes:* * In each cell, the estimated regression parameters and the standard deviations are denoted, respectively.

*Source:* IMF staff estimates.

Most of the coefficient signs are as hypothesised above, with many of them statistically significant (*t*-values in brackets), and the goodness of fit, measured by the adjusted $R^2$ statistic, is very high, being no less than 0.48 and ranging up to almost 0.80.

Before we go on to discuss the results for individual variables in the model, we note that factor expansion – which usually plays a large role in statistical studies of long-term growth in other economies proxied by the investment ratio – was not found to show a significant statistical association with growth in this study (results not shown). This confirms the results of Wolf, who even found a negative effect of investment on growth.[36] Although it should be recalled that investment data are particularly weak, this seems to suggest that so far the recovery in transition economies has not depended as much on new investment as on a reallocation of existing resources. The nature of transition is such that efficiency improvements are an important source of early growth. The impact of resource reallocation will of course be temporary and over time growth will come to depend on the more traditional factors, such as the expansion of physical and human capital. In this connection, we may note that foreign direct investment (FDI), which is sometimes thought to be an easy solution to stimulate growth, only gives statistically significant results when structural reforms are not accounted for in the model specification, and even then its association with growth is much weaker than that of reforms. When the reform index is included in the specification, we find no significant effect of FDI on growth. Although one can observe a broad association – better performing economies have more FDI – this may actually reflect a reverse causation. That is, the same factors that promote growth (stabilisation, reforms) also attract FDI and hence the strong correlation between structural reforms and FDI.[37]

*Table 3.4  Growth determinants: panel estimates for subperiods (1990–1993) and (1994–1997)*[*]

| | | | Independent variables | | | | |
|---|---|---|---|---|---|---|---|
| | LNP | RI | LIP | LEN | LEX | LEG | R² Adj. |
| Time period 1990–1993 | | | | | | | |
| 3.B1 | −2.08 | 2.51 | | | | | |
| | −12.00 | 1.53 | | | | | 0.48 |
| 3.B2 | −1.91 | 13.75 | −12.40 | | | | |
| | −11.01 | 2.99 | −2.58 | | | | 0.53 |
| 3.B3 | −2.00 | | 1.38 | | | | |
| | −11.67 | | 0.82 | | | | 0.51 |
| 3.B4 | −2.09 | −0.81 | | 4.42 | | | |
| | −12.00 | −0.27 | | 11.15 | | | 0.48 |
| 3.B5 | | | | 3.52 | | | |
| | | | | 1.76 | | | 0.49 |
| 3.B6 | −2.02 | −3.03 | | | 4.08 | | |
| | −11.36 | −0.57 | | | 1.09 | | 0.50 |
| 3.B7 | −2.08 | | | | 2.28 | | |
| | −12.70 | | | | 1.67 | | 0.48 |
| Time period 1994–1997 | | | | | | | |
| 3.C1 | −2.44 | 14.11 | | | | | |
| | 16.05 | 21.12 | | | | | 0.81 |
| 3.C2 | −2.84 | 3.01 | −12.47 | | | | |
| | −11.88 | 1.10 | 3.45 | | | | 0.77 |
| 3.C3 | −2.30 | | 16.00 | | | | |
| | −14.04 | | 17.15 | | | | 0.76 |
| 3.C4 | −2.64 | 13.08 | | −0.43 | | | |
| | −12.21 | 3.73 | | −0.12 | | | 0.74 |
| 3.C5 | −2.30 | | | 13.91 | | | |
| | −16.01 | | | 20.41 | | | 0.80 |
| 3.C6 | −2.39 | 5.75 | | | 6.08 | | |
| | −13.47 | 1.38 | | | 1.93 | | 0.75 |
| 3.C7 | −2.34 | | | | 10.26 | | |
| | −13.00 | | | | 16.73 | | 0.74 |
| 3.C8 | −2.05 | 15.37 | | | | −2.25 | |
| | −12.34 | 10.08 | | | | −1.97 | 0.87 |
| 3.C9 | −1.42 | | | | | 9.78 | |
| | −6.77 | | | | | 12.91 | 0.74 |

*Note:*   [*] The independent variables are listed in the columns of the table. In each cell, the estimated regression parameters and the standard deviations are denoted, respectively. Reform Index (*RI*) excludes subcomponent when subcomponent is included separately in the specification.

*Source*:  IMF staff estimates.

## Role of Principal Policy Variables

As expected, the coefficient for *inflation* is negative (Figure 3.1). Finding
that inflation is bad for growth is neither new nor surprising; to explore this
effect further on the importance of disinflation, we have also tried to
determine at what level inflation starts to have a significant adverse effect on
growth.[38] To do this, we added dummies to the most basic equation 3.A1,
with the dummies having a value of 1 when inflation is above a certain
threshold, and a value of 0 otherwise. Subsequently we estimated the
equation using various levels of inflation as the breaking point. We found
that the dummy becomes statistically significant (at the 5 per cent level) with
a negative sign at a rate of inflation of 31 per cent. An alternative test, where
the dummies have a value of 1 when inflation is below a certain threshold,
found a significant positive coefficient for values below 22 per cent. This
suggests that inflation levels higher than the range of 20–30 per cent
significantly hurt growth.[39]

These higher values for transition countries may themselves be
'transitional'. That is, transition economies beginning a successful
stabilisation combined with a good beginning on reforms may induce growth
simply by pushing inflation from very high levels to well below 100 per cent.
But unless the trend continues – lower inflation, more reforms – growth may
stall, as it did in Albania, Bulgaria and Romania.[40] The fact that the two tests
do not yield the same cut-off point suggests that the relationship between
inflation and growth is a non-linear one.

Structural reforms have a particularly strong and positive overall impact on
growth. Consistent with earlier empirical results, when lagged values of the
reform index are added, we find that the effect of reforms occurs over a
longer period.[41] In fact growth appears to be negatively affected by the level
of contemporaneous reforms. However, this is quickly compensated if
reforms continue, and on balance growth is affected positively by the
accumulated stock of reforms (indicated by the sum of the coefficients).
Thus, reforms have an initial cost, but this is more than offset in following
years. Reforms foster resource reallocation as well as investment in physical
and human capital, both of which take time to yield positive effects on
economic performance. By not including the lag structure for the reform
index, one would miss this initial adverse effect on growth and misrepresent
the short- and long-run effects of structural reforms.

The statistical association between growth on the one hand, and inflation
and structural reforms on the other, is quite strong. In the econometric
results, about 70 per cent of the variation in output is explained by these two
factors alone (equation 3.A2). Countries with better growth performance had
generally lower inflation and a higher degree of progressive structural
reforms. The relationship is also fairly robust; estimating specifications with

different lag structures and/or adding or eliminating other variables does not affect the statistical significance much, nor does it result in a much different magnitude of the steady-state effect of both variables on growth.

*Figure 3.1 The impact of inflation on growth*

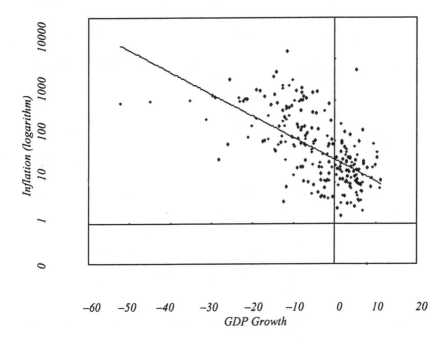

*Source*: National Authorities and IMF staff estimates.

Next we turn to analyse whether some *elements of reforms* are more important than others. Indices for individual components of structural reforms were added or substituted for the overall reform index. When individual components were added to, the overall index was corrected for these components. The subindices include an index for internal price liberalisation (*LIP*), private entry in markets (comprising privatisation, enterprise reform and financial sector reform (*LEN*), liberalisation of the trade and exchange regimes (*LEX*), and legal reform (*LEG*, only available for the 1995–97 period).[42]

We do not find that adding the various reform subcomponents, or substituting them for the overall index, improved the explanatory power. We find that price liberalisation has an initial negative impact on growth, while its lagged values have a positive effect. Thus, price liberalisation initially has a 'destructive' effect, as existing enterprises find it harder to compete, while new enterprises take time to develop. Berg et al., using a full period specification and time lags, also found these negative effects for current year price liberalisation in some regressions but not in those which include initial conditions.[43] Hernández-Catá finds, as we do, stronger evidence for the early 'pain' of price liberalisation.[44] Enterprise reform also appears to have a negative contemporaneous effect on growth, while lagged values show a positive association, reflecting that enterprises need time to restructure. Trade and exchange reform has an immediate positive effect on growth.

The effect of large governments on growth, which has been given less attention in the literature, is negative and significant. This seems to suggest, as Kornai posited, that the recession is not a Keynesian one as long as soft budgets continue, and/or that any government spending impulse that stimulates growth is at most temporary and is outweighed by the adverse effects of large bureaucracies, high tax rates and crowding-out. However, we found that the impact of the size of the government is less important than stabilisation and structural reforms. Still, the econometric results suggest that each percentage point decline in the ratio of government expenditure to GDP results in 0.10–0.25 per cent higher annual growth.

The size of the government can be expected to affect economic performance in transition economies along the following channels. A market economy has three main components: (i) enterprises; (ii) markets; and (iii) the institutions allowing markets to work. How well these components work and interact depends very much on the role the government plays in the economy. In most transition economies, particularly in the CIS, the role of the government in each of these three components is, albeit to a varying degree, still significant. Typically, expenditures are tilted heavily towards unproductive sectors, such as subsidies to enterprises, a large bureaucracy, and an untargeted social safety net. This diversion of so many resources to government-funded activities is itself an impediment to growth. Beyond this, the continued interference of the government in many aspects of economic life as well as deficiencies in the institutional framework create serious obstacles to the development of a favourable business climate and the realisation of the country's economic potential. The counterpart of the large size of the government is a heavy tax burden, which is an additional factor deterring the development of the enterprise sector. The high tax rates create an incentive to conceal production or to increase the use of barter transactions, which not only drive economic activity to the shadow economy, but in so doing discourage expansion of this activity. Adding to the tax burden on enterprises are 'unofficial' taxes, as government officials try to supplement their low wages by requiring side-payments from enterprises for services rendered, such as the granting of licences. In addition, the inability to reduce government expenditures substantially has caused budget deficits to remain relatively high, the financing of which crowds out the enterprise sector.

## Decline Period versus Recovery Period

Apart from estimating the relationship between growth, disinflation and (components of) structural reforms for the entire period, the data set was also broken down into two subperiods. Although somewhat arbitrary, it is useful to consider the period of 'decline' (1990–93), during which at most a handful of countries had seen the beginnings of recovery; and the period of 'recovery' (1994–97) during which nearly a dozen countries experienced three or more years of growth and most others either began to grow or at least saw the decline approaching bottom.

It is notable that the explanatory power, the statistical significance (*t*-values), and even size of coefficients for the reform variables, is higher in panel C of Table 3.4, that is, for the 1994–97 period, which can be considered as the recovery period.[45] The stronger results for reform variables in the second period compared to the first period can be interpreted as saying that at first the effect of reforms in helping slow the decline is positive but mild, but over time, as reforms continue, their cumulative effect strengthens and leads to recovery or positive growth. This phenomenon is well illustrated by Figure 3.2, showing the predicted relation between growth and degree of reforms in the two subperiods. It shows that in the early period 1990–93, reforms had a 'U-curve' effect: limited reforms helped prevent a strong decline in output, while very strong reforms did not preclude decline, but that decline was not as great as for intermediate reformers. Once the early decline was overcome, however, the effect of reforms on growth for the 1994–97 period was unequivocally favourable. Those with the strongest reforms were the best performers; those with least reform did most poorly.

When the estimation period is divided into two, we find that price liberalisation has an adverse effect on growth in the early years, while it has a clear positive effect in the later years (Table 3.4, equation 3.B2 versus 3.C2). This supports the notion that price liberalisation has an initial destructive effect. Trade and exchange liberalisation has a significant positive effect in the recovery period. Otherwise we find that the subindices are each close substitutes for the general index, but do not have additional separate significance in the statistical analysis. The generally very close association of the various subcomponents of reform is similar to the results for non-transition economies in Aziz and Wescott, namely that it is a *combination* of policies that is more critical for growth than any single type of policy.[46]

*Good Governance in Central and Eastern Europe*

*Figure 3.2   The impact of reform on growth: fitted regression values*\*

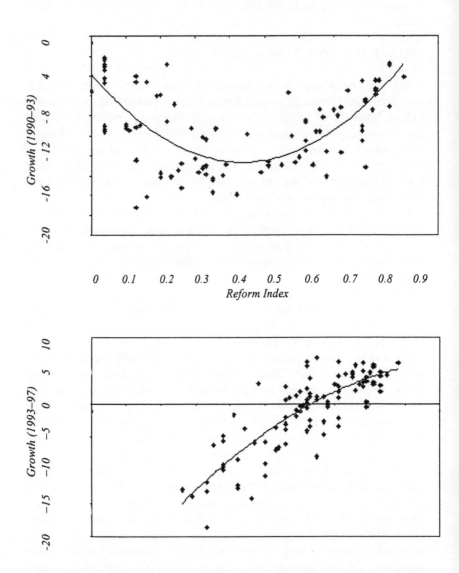

*Notes*:   \* The fitted values are obtained from the multivariate panel data regression
3.B1 from Table 3.4 (top part) and 3.C1 from Table 3.4 (bottom part). A
polynomial trend line has been added for the fitted regression.

*Source*: Author's estimates and European Bank for Reconstruction and Development,
*Transition Report* (London 1997).

## Role of Initial Conditions

There is a negative association between economic growth and the variables capturing the initial macroeconomic and structural conditions (Table 3.3, equations (3.A4)–(3.A10)). These findings are consistent with those of de Melo et al.[47] Contrary to their results, however, we find here that the negative effect of initial structural conditions – including elements such as level of per capita income, overindustrialisation and urbanisation – is statistically stronger than that of initial macroeconomic conditions. The coefficient of *INCOND1* is of the wrong sign and not statistically significant in equations that include inflation (equation (3.A3) versus equation (3.A7)). Individual components such as the (deviation from the average) degree of industrialisation and initial per capita income also show an adverse association with growth (equations (3.A6), (3.A9) and (3.A10)), although the level of industrialisation is not statistically significant when inflation is included. The results using individual components are very similar to those using the clusters representing various initial conditions (equation (3.A9) versus (3.A7)). The specifications we used presuppose that initial conditions continue to have the same effect throughout the transition period, which might be too strong an assumption; it would seem reasonable to expect that the effect of adverse initial conditions would diminish over time. Berg et al. test for this effect and do find a decline over time.[48] When we included a linear transformation of the degree of industrialisation ($IDT = ID/t$ with $t = 1$, ..., 8) that imposes a declining weight over time on the initial degree of industrialisation, we found the statistical significance of this variable to be stronger than that of the level of industrialisation itself.

To assess the relative importance of policies versus initial conditions, we first followed the methodology applied by de Melo et al., which uses the adjusted $R^2$ to determine the contribution of each group of variables to the total variation explained by the complete set of factors.[49] We find that policies – macroeconomic, structural – and the size of the government, account for about 95 per cent of the total variation explained, while initial conditions account for only 5 per cent. The latter is considerably lower than what de Melo et al. found, but their specification did not include a variable representing macroeconomic policies. From this we may conclude that policies are the most important factor explaining differences in growth performance between countries.

As an alternative approach, we posed the same question as a trade-off between unfavourable initial conditions and more reforms. We calculated what it would require in terms of additional structural reforms to offset the effects of relatively more adverse initial conditions. Our findings imply that, if countries do suffer from an unfavourable starting point, it requires relatively little effort from structural policies to compensate for this. Using for example either equation (3.A9) or (3.A10), it can be calculated that the adverse impact of a 10 per cent of GDP higher degree of industrialisation can be offset by increasing the intensity of reforms by only 0.04 on a scale between 0 and 1. We also compared CIS countries with the countries in Central and Eastern Europe. Equation (3.A4) suggests that the negative impact of the relatively more adverse initial situation in CIS countries could be offset by increasing the reform index by only 0.06. For the western CIS countries, which suffered more from a higher degree of over-industrialisation, the additional reform effort would be to increase the index by 0.15. Alternatively, to compensate for the relatively worse initial conditions, the average size of the government in CIS countries would need to be reduced by about 6 per cent of GDP. Of course, combinations of both policy responses could be chosen as well to achieve the same result. For a country such as – for example – Ukraine, the relatively more unfavourable initial conditions compared with other CIS countries could be overcome by stepping up structural reforms so as to increase the reform index from a level of 0.57 in 1997 to 0.65. The latter is comparable to the level of more advanced reformers in the CIS, such as Kazakhstan.

The model specification describes economic performance in the former Soviet Union countries or CIS countries equally well as that in the countries of Central and Eastern Europe; when dummies (*FSUDUM*) for either one of these groups were added to equation (3.A4), they were found to be insignificant (equation (3.A6)).[50] This confirms the earlier findings of Berg et al.[51] Only when a variable capturing macroeconomic policies is omitted from the specification do we find dummy variables for the former Soviet Union or CIS countries to be statistically significant (equation (3.A8)). This underlines the important role of macroeconomic policies in explaining differences in economic performance.

## CONCLUSION

The chapter has analysed the growth performance of 25 transition countries in the 1990–97 period, attempting to relate it statistically to the main factors which are thought to promote recovery and sustained growth: initial conditions, stabilisation and structural reforms. The econometric analysis, utilising a larger data set then most earlier studies, demonstrates that compact 'stylised facts' specifications turn out to have nearly as much explanatory power and statistical significance as more elaborate specifications. The results broadly confirm not only expectations based on theory, but also the results of several preceding studies; that is, macroeconomic stabilisation and structural reforms are the key to the economic recovery. Growth performance is clearly better where stabilisation has been achieved earliest and where structural reforms have progressed the most. In the category of structural reforms, we find that there is no single simple reform that provides a magic solution for growth; rather, it is a combined package of reforms that is needed; it is 'the thousand and one little daily improvements' of Harberger that bring results.[52] A crucial component of this reform package, which has not been explicitly tested in earlier statistical work, is the reduction of government size and expenditures. Our analysis demonstrates the positive and statistically significant effect of a reduction in the size of the government on economic performance.

The impact of structural reforms on growth is different in the decline and recovery phases, with clear evidence of some 'pain' at the beginning of reform. We find that in the early period, 1990–93, when most of the 25 countries experienced output decline, reforms had a 'U-curve' effect: limited reforms helped prevent a strong decline in output, intermediate reforms resulted in a stronger output decline, while very strong reforms did not preclude decline, but that decline was not as great as for intermediate reformers. Once the early decline was overcome, however, the effect of reforms on recovery and positive growth for the 1994–97 period was unequivocally favourable. Those with the greatest amount of reform were the best performers; those with least reform did most poorly.

As far as the effects of unfavourable initial conditions on economic performance are concerned, the study confirms earlier findings that a higher degree of the distortions that were characteristic of the Soviet period acted as a deterrent to growth and recovery. However, the magnitude of this effect was found to be very small in comparison with the other factors affecting growth and its retarding effect on growth is easily compensated by a modest acceleration of structural reforms.

Indeed, given the clearly substantial achievements in stabilising inflation in the majority of transition countries, the most important additional measures in promoting growth are a combination of reducing government size, and stepping up progress on structural reforms. As this is done, however, sustaining growth will also require continued effort to reduce inflation levels to low single digits. While the early success of bringing inflation down to low double digits may have been enough to permit the first shoots of economic growth to sprout, as the transition progresses the threshold at which inflation hurts growth will fall to the levels found for market economies, which is well below 10 per cent.[53] Not only is inflation control not a magic elixir leading to growth: the effort to control inflation must be sustained permanently.

The quest for good policies which promote growth must recognise that, as Fischer writes, 'it is a long and arduous task, a matter of many people doing many things right, over many years, to make a country grow'.[54]

# NOTES

1. The views expressed in the chapter are those of the authors and do not represent the position or official views of the International Monetary Fund.
2. On catch-up, see Stanley Fischer, Ratna Sahay and Carlos A. Végh, 'The Process of Socialist Economic Transformation', *Journal of Economic Perspectives*, 5, 4 (1996) pp. 91–105 and Jeffrey Sachs and Andrew M. Warner, 'Achieving Rapid Growth in the Transition Economies of Central Europe', Stockholm Institute of East European Economies, Working Paper, 116 (1996). The former, for example, calculate that with a per capita growth rate of 4.75 per cent annually it would take on average 35 years to catch up to the average level of the countries belonging to the Organisation for Economic Cooperation and Development (OECD). With a growth rate of 4 per cent it would take 45 years.
3. Albania, Bulgaria, Croatia, the Czech Republic, Estonia, Hungary, Latvia, Lithuania, the Former Yugoslav Republic of Macedonia (FYROM), Poland, Romania, the Slovak Republic and Slovenia.
4 Armenia, Azerbaijan, Belarus, Georgia, Kazakhstan, the Kyrgyz Republic, Moldova, the Russian Federation, Tajikistan, Turkmenistan, Ukraine and Uzbekistan.
5. We use the reform index constructed by Martha de Melo, Cevdet Denizer and Alan Gelb, 'From Plan to Market: Patterns of Transition', World Bank, Policy Research Department, Transition Economics Division (Washington 1996) for the years 1990–93, updated to 1997 by linking it to the transition indicators of the European Bank for Reconstruction and Development (EBRD).
6. Through 1995, for 25 countries, one would have 35 observations with positive growth of a total 125 observations; through 1996 this would be 54 of 175, while including 1997 gives 74 of 200.
7. See, for example, Marcelo Selowsky and Ricardo Martin, 'Policy Performance and Output Growth in the Transition Economies', The Transition from Socialism, *American Economic Association Papers and Proceedings*, 87, 2 (1996) pp. 349–53 and Jeffrey Sachs, 'The Transition at Mid Decade', Economic Transition in Central and Eastern Europe, *American Economic Association Papers and Proceedings*, 86, 2 (1996) pp. 128–33.
8. Martha de Melo et al., 'Circumstance and Choice: The Role of Initial Conditions and Policies in Transition Economies', International Finance Corporation (Washington DC 1997) and Andrew Berg et al., 'The Evolution of Output in Transition Economies: Explaining the Differences', *IMF Working Paper* (Washington DC 1999)
9. This set was synthasized in Paul Romer, 'Endogenous Technological Change', *Journal of Political Economy*, 98, 5 (1990) pp. 71–102 and Robert J. Barro and Xavier Sala-i-Martin, *Economic Growth* (New York 1995).
10. Mancur Olson, 'Distinguished Lecture on Economics in Government: "Big Bills Left on the Sidewalk: Why Some Nations are Rich and Others Poor"', *Journal of Economic Perspectives*, 10 (1997) pp. 3–24.
11. The list is long and we note here a central example: Robert J. Barro, *Determinants of Economic Growth: A Cross-country Empirical Study* (Cambridge MA 1997). As the authors of these many studies themselves warn, all of these results,

however plausible, need to be interpreted with caution due to the measurement and methodology problems involved, not least because many of the variables used are likely to be highly correlated. The pitfalls are well reflected in a recent paper by Xavier Sala-i-Martin, 'I Just Ran Four Million Regressions', NBER Working Paper, 6252, National Bureau of Economic Research (Cambridge MA 1997).

12. Michael Bruno and William Easterly, 'Inflation Crises and Long-Run Growth', *Journal of Monetary Economics*, 41 (1998) suggest the higher range. Others, such as Stanley Fischer, 'The role of Macroeconomic Factors in Growth', *Journal of Monetary Economics,* 32 (1993), Michael Sarel, 'Nonlinear Effects of Inflation on Economic Growth', *IMF Staff Papers* 43 (1996), Atish Ghosh and Steven Phillips, 'Inflation, Disinflation, and Growth', IMF Working Paper, 98/68, International Monetary Fund (Washington DC 1998), find the breaking point to be much lower. Later in the chapter we report on some results from transition economies.

13. János Kornai, 'Tranformational Recession: The Main Causes', *Journal of Comparative Economics*, 19 (1994) pp. 39–63.

14. Oliver Blanchard, *The Economics of Transition in Eastern Europe* (Oxford 1997).

15. European Bank for Reconstruction and Development, Transition Report (London 1997) provides an excellent review of the conceptual framework in the 'creative destruction' spirit, as well as empirical analysis of such changes in the transition so far.

16. Stanley Fischer and Alan Gelb, 'The Process of Socialist Economic Transformation', *Journal of Economic Perspectives*, 5, 4 (1991) pp. 91–105.

17. It should be clear that while net aggregate investment need not be high to promote recovery, the reallocation to new sectors and products could allow for large net investment in the growing areas while the old ones experience negative net investment. Recent studies of survey data suggest that even at the firm level, very high productivity growth is seen during the transition. See Gerhard Pohl et al., 'Privatization and Restructuring in Central and Eastern Europe: Evidence and Policy Options', World Bank Technical Paper, 368 (Washington DC 1997).

18. Oleh Havrylyshyn and Peter Botousharov, 'Five Years of Transition', Bank Review, 4, Bulgarian National Bank (Sofia 1995) and Fischer, Sahay and Végh, 'The Process of Socialist Economic Transformation'.

19. See Sachs, 'The Transition at Mid Decade'; Selowsky and Martin, 'Policy Performance and Output Growth'.

20. See Anders Åslund et al., 'How to Stabilize: Lessons from Post-Communist countries', *Brookings Papers on Economic Activity*: 1 (1996) pp. 217–313; Fischer and Végh, 'The Process of Socialist Economic Transformation'; Ernesto Hernández-Catá, 'Liberalization and the Behavior of Output During the Transition from Plan to Market', IMF Working Paper, 97/53, International Monetary Fund (Washington DC 1997); de Melo et. al., 'Circumstance and Choice'; Berg et al., 'The Evolution of Output'.

21. Günter Taube and Jeromin Zettelmeyer, 'Output Decline and Recovery in Uzbekistan: Past Performance and Future Prospects', IMF Working Paper, (Washington DC 1999).

22. See Åslund et al., 'How to Stabilize' and Philippe Aghion and Oliver Jean Blanchard, 'On the speed of Transition in Central Europe', EBRD Working Paper, 6, European Bank for Reconstruction and Development (London 1993).
23. De Melo et al., 'Circumstance and Choice'; Åslund, et al. 'How to Stabilize'.
24. Berg et al., 'The Evolution of Output'.
25. Yet a third way of looking at this is to hypothesise that initial conditions play an indirect role through the politics of determining how committed a government is to stabilise and undertake structural reforms. Holger C. Wolf, Transition Strategies: Choices and Outcomes, unpublished manuscript, Stern Business School (New York 1997) takes this approach.
26. Aymo Brunetti, Gregory Kisunko and Betrice Weder, 'Credibility of Rules and Economic Growth: Evidence From a Worldwide Survey of th Private Sector', Policy Research Working Paper, 1760, World Bank (Washington DC 1997); Simon Johnson, Daniel Kaufman and Andrei Shleifer, 'The Unofficial Economy in Transition', *Brookings Papers on Economic Activity*, 2; Mancur Olson, Naveen Sarna and Anand V. Swamy, 'Governance and Growth: A Simple Hypothesis Explaining Cross-Country Differences in Productivity Growth', a draft paper for the Center of Economic Growth of the United States Agency forInternational Developmetn (Washington 1997).
27. Arnold C. Harberger, 'A Vision of the Growth Process', *The American Economic Review*, 88, 1 (1998) pp. 1–32.
28. Johnson et al., 'The Unofficial Economy' provide the most comprehensive set of estimates of the unofficial economy for 17 countries over the period 1989–95. They show values ranging from 5 to 13 per cent in Slovakia, the Czech Republic, Poland and Estonia, to 50 to 60 per cent in Ukraine, Georgia and Azerbaijan.
29. Including: repressed inflation, black market premium, trade dependency, market memory, existence as an independent state prior to 1989 and location.
30. Including: 1989 per capita income, the level of urbanisation and over-industrialisation, prior economic growth and the richness of natural resources.
31. De Melo et al., 'From Plan to Market'; European Bank for Reconstruction and Development, transition Report (London, various years).
32. De Melo et al., 'Circumstance and Choice'.
33. Barro, Determinants of Economic Growth; Barro and Sala-i-Martin, *Economic Growth*.
34. Kornai, 'Transformational Recession'.
35. De Melo et al., 'Circumstance and Choice'.
36. Wolf, 'Transition Strategies'.
37. As other empirical studies, we also were unable to find a statistically significant association for openness trade to GDP ratio. This may reflect a problem of trade data especially in early years, or a difficulty with this simple measure of trade openness which does not control for the size of an economy. International Monetary Fund, 'Growth Experiences in Transition Economies', SM, 98/228 (Washington DC 1998) does, however, report a non-econometric result of a broad association for groups of countries. Those with a more sustained growth record tend to have higher growth rates of export than those with very recent growth, or no growth, or reversals.
38. As noted above, this was the earliest important conclusion in studies of growth in transition and the least controversial; our results merely affirm that this effect still

holds, despite the fact that a few countries have attained low inflation without seeing recovery. Ukraine and to some extent Turkmenistan are examples, but they also serve to make the point that stabilisation, while necessary, may not be sufficient for growth.

39. Our result is consistent with the findings of Bruno and Easterly, 'Inflation Crises and Long-Run Growth'. Others, such as Fischer, 'The Role of Macroeconomic Factors in Growth'; Sarel, 'Nonlineair Effects of Inflation' and Ghosh and Phillips, 'Inflation, Disinflation, and Growth' find the threshold to be much lower (6 to 10 per cent), although these studies did not include transition economies. Another study, by Peter Christoffersen and Peter Doyle, 'From Inflation to Growth', finds a value of 13 per cent.

40. In IMF, 'Growth Experiences in Transition Economies' it is argued that the cases of Belarus and Uzbekistan are analogous to Bulgaria and Romania in the use of directed credits to stimulate growth. As noted above, Taube and Zettelmeyer, 'Output Decline and Recovery', explain at least part of the Uzbekistan puzzle by its reliance on cotton exports.

41. See de Melo et al., 'From Plan to Market'; Selowsky and Martin, 'Policy Performance and Output'; de Melo et al., 'Circumstance and Choice'; Wolf, 'Transition Strategies'.

42. Again, these indices are due to de Melo et al., 'From Plan to Market', for the years 1990–93, updated until 1997 using the transition indicators from the European Bank for Reconstruction and Development, Transition Reports.

43. Berg et al., 'The Evolution of Output'.

44. Hernández-Catá, 'Liberalization and the Behaviour of Output'.

45. Because of the short estimation periods, no lagged values of the reform index were included in the specification. Hence, no distinction can be made between the first-year effect of reforms and the effects in subsequent years.

46. Jahangir Aziz and Robert F. Wescott, 'Policy Complementaries and the Washington Consensus', IMF Working Paper, 97/118, International Monetary Fund (Washington 1997).

47. De Melo et al., 'Circumstance and Choice'.

48. Berg et al., 'The Evolution of Output'.

49. De Melo et al. 'Circumstance and Choice'.

50. A CIS dummy provided the same results.

51. Berg et al., 'The Evolution of Output'.

52. Haberger, 'A Vision of the Growth Process'.

53. See Ghosh and Phillips, 'Inflation, Disinflation, and Growth', for a recent econometric study on this and a review of other works; the range is from as low as 3 per cent to not higher than 8 per cent.

54. Stanley Fischer, 'ABCDE: Tenth Conference Address', speech presented at the World Bank Annual Bank Conference on Development Economies (Washington DC April 1998).

# 4. Governance, Conditionality and Transformation in Post-socialist Countries

## Joachim Ahrens

### INTRODUCTION

In the 1990s, governance has come to be a prominent policy concern of bilateral and multilateral development organisations. Increasingly, donor agencies have considered governance issues as critical for sustained development and systemic transformation and seek to explore ways to incorporate governance-related components into their aid policies. This appears to be a particularly important issue with respect to post-socialist countries (PSCs).[1] Being in the midst of their transition toward democratic societies and market-orientated economies, the state is subject to a fundamental reorientation. On the one hand, it is required to reduce its role in the economy and to abandon its interference into private actions. On the other hand, the state needs to assume new roles in order to enhance and preserve markets. New institutions need to be crafted which improve the capability and the capacity of the state to implement public policies and to facilitate private sector co-ordination.

However, there are still no clear or settled ideas about how effective governance should be suitably defined, let alone how key governance issues can be appropriately incorporated into externally-financed programmes of policy reform. This chapter aims at contributing to this debate from a political-economy point of view and seeks to explore ways in which multilateral development banks (the World Bank and the European Bank for Reconstruction and Development (EBRD)) and the International Monetary Fund (IMF) can effectively incorporate governance issues in their efforts to support governments in PSCs.[2] The main argument of the chapter is that negative or punitive measures – that is, politically-conditioned aid, to foster governance – will be less effective and meet stronger political resistance than positive measures which reward efforts to improve governance structures. Multilateral donors should refrain from imposing political conditions and instead seek to improve governance structures in close co-ordination and co-operation with governments of the recipient countries, which need to assume full ownership of reforms.

The remainder of the chapter is organised as follows. In the next section, a concept of governance is developed that may represent a suitable institutional foundation of economic policy reform in transition countries. Attention then turns to the need to strengthen governance structures in Central and Eastern Europe (CEE) and the Commonwealth of Independent States (CIS) and the current approaches of the multilateral financial organisations to governance-related problems. Finally comes the question of whether or not a new kind of conditionality is required in international lending operations.

## WHAT IS EFFECTIVE GOVERNANCE?

A pivotal purpose of the state is to provide public goods, create and sustain social benefits, conduct public policies that add to collective welfare, and craft the institutional environment in which markets operate. But its potential will only be realised if authorities are credibly committed to managing the state in the collective interest and if institutions are in place which shape the incentives of political actors accordingly. As Leonard says: 'Just as with the collectively owned field, if those who control the state continuously use it only to maximise their own narrow, individual interests, they will soon run it down and it will produce less and less benefit for society as a whole'.[3]

Today, there is a heightened awareness across both the donor community and governments of recipient countries that the quality of a country's *governance structure* is a key determinant of the ability to pursue sustainable economic and social development. But, as yet, students of development and policy makers have not agreed upon an unambiguous and operational definition of the term. Instead, a confusing variety of definitions, which greatly differ with respect to issues, problems, or objectives, can be found in current development debates. For instance, Frischtak defines governance capacity 'as the ability to co-ordinate the aggregation of diverging interests and thus promote policy that can credibly be taken to represent the public interest'; Bratton and van de Walle interpret governance as 'an interactive process by which state and social actors reciprocally probe for a consensus on the rules of the political game', while Hydén views governance as 'the conscious management of regime structures with a view to enhancing the legitimacy of the public realm'.[4]

The term is often used as a buzzword in political discussions. Some users of the term either do not offer any definition or seek to incorporate too many aspects so that the underlying concept turns out to be useless for the purposes of policy reform.[5] Some definitions prove to be completely redundant: if governance is perceived as *good government*, for example.[6] Other uses of the term highlight several substantive characteristics of a governance concept but do not offer a proper definition. The recent literature on obstacles to structural adjustment addresses several critical elements for a suitable conceptualisation of the term, but does not explicitly refer to the notion of governance.[7] Several scholars interpret governance as an end in itself, while others see it as an analytical framework or as a means to promote sustainable development.[8]

Some approaches seek to conceptualise the term by addressing aspects which are critical from the perspective of policy reform, but the underlying definitions are vague and hardly operational for practical purposes. This is the flavour of the definition used by the World Bank, which defines governance as 'the manner in which power is exercised in the management of a country's economic and social resources for development. Good governance (...) is synonymous with sound development management'.[9] A more operational definition, suitable for improving the practice of policy making in PSCs, may be derived from conceptual considerations, which address key issues of policy reform.[10]

One conceptual approach to governance views democratisation as an unalterable prerequisite for sustained economic adjustment. Effective governance then corresponds to democracy that not only keeps government small, but also ensures that economics dominates over politics. Because of the assumption that democracy may provide a remedy against a big and potentially corrupt government, democratic institutions and processes are regarded as effective devices to secure emerging markets. However, the concept of democracy seems to be too broad for a proper operationalisation of the term. Furthermore, the derived thesis that democracy will automatically foster economic growth and development is not well supported empirically.[11] Hence, one may agree with Frischtak, who states that '(t)o build attributes to specific political regimes into the very concept of governance – quite apart from the fact that these attributes and norms may be worth promoting in their own right – detracts from the analytical utility and credibility of the concept'.[12]

Another conceptual underpinning to governance identifies the institutional capacities of state apparatuses as the crucial constraint to successful policy reform. This approach circumvents the debate on big versus small government and, instead, focuses on specific characteristics of government machinery such as autonomy, rationality, efficiency and technocratic capability which make public administrations less dependent on the disruptions of politics. Indeed, institution building has been increasingly recognised by the development community as a key ingredient of policy reform. This conception highlights some of the key constraints faced by adjusting states. But it will unfold its inherent potential to improve our understanding of the political economy of policy reform only if it can (i) succeed in identifying the conditions which will allow states to develop the required institutional capacity; and (ii) adequately incorporate state–society relations in its analytical framework.

The third conception worth noting adds the dimension of informal institutions (culture, habits, traditions), which shape individual behaviour and subjective perceptions, to the governance framework.[13] The policy prescriptions associated with this approach include that both development strategies and reform policies ought to be compatible with cultural characteristics and that effective governance needs to take into consideration the belief systems persisting in society[14] This line of reasoning adds an important aspect to the discussion on governance, one which has usually been neglected by the economics profession. It also implies that, because development is path dependent, there is no universal model of effective governance to be successfully applied to all PSCs.

This conception may be of particular importance for the systemic transformation of PSCs. For, as several scholars have argued, the transition towards capitalism may be impeded by informal institutions which evolved in PSCs before and during socialist rule.[15] These include widespread pro-collectivist attitudes, nationalism, communalism, and habituation to political hierarchy. The philosophical heritage has not been conducive either to individualism or to performance-contingent rewards or to a constitutional state. As Pejovich says that '(P)eople see the gains from exchange as a redistribution of wealth within the community rather than as rewards for creating new value'.[16] Also, many East Europeans did not perceive capitalism as a system based on self-responsibility, self-determination and competition, but rather as a system automatically providing a great variety of goods and large incomes, the realisation of which would require neither reducing 'socialist' welfare benefits nor changing the traditional work ethos. Therefore, as Pejovich ays, 'the transition process was a crude awakening that capitalism is not merely about being rich'.[17] These factors made the transformation process path dependent and induced hysteresis effects, so that capitalist behavioural norms as postulated by neoclassical reasoning could not emerge in the short run. This also means that creating capitalist institutions by fiat following textbook models will not yield the intended effects. It also implies acceptance problems, as the resurgence of pro-collectivist political parties indicates. Instead, policy makers should seek citizens' compliance to transformation policies by allowing them to experiment with alternative institutions and to adopt those arrangements that pass the market test. A market for institutions (for example, regarding the choice of contractual agreements and the design of property-rights structures)[18] in association with the transfer of productive assets to non-elites would provide the underprivileged with upward mobility, help to overcome hysteresis effects, and encourage a consensus for the support of economic reforms.

Finally, a fourth conception, which is closely related to problems of policy reform, views governance as an approach that comprises the establishment of abstract, universal rules, their enforcement mechanisms, and also stable and transparent mechanisms of conflict resolution. This conception refrains from making any normative judgement concerning specific political regimes and rather follows Weber's notion of the modern state.[19] Weber proposed that the operation of markets requires a high degree of calculability based on legal rationality, the rational administration of justice, and a relatively insulated bureaucracy (characterised by a functional definition of duties and full-time devotion to administrative tasks), whose work is not only based on instrumental rationality, but essentially on the development and enforcement of universal legal norms. Similar to Weber, who conceived that his ideal type of state is most conducive to the functioning of modern capitalist societies, this conception also suggests that its notion of governance is the key to creating an enabling environment for policy making and business activities.

The definition of governance which is considered appropriate for the purposes of this chapter is based on the conclusions which can be drawn from the above conceptions. Hence, governance is defined as the capacity of the formal and informal institutional environment (in which individual actors, social groups, civic organisations and policy-makers interact with one another) to implement and enforce public policies and to improve private sector co-ordination. In that sense, governance *per se* is neither good nor bad. But in its concrete form a governance structure – the underlying institutional environment (comprising formal and informal political, economic and social institutions) as realised in a particular country – may increase the efficacy of policy reform or prove to be harmful for economic and social development. Governance, as defined above, is not an end in itself but a means to implement and enforce feasible policies properly. A governance structure affects the incentives of politicians, bureaucrats and private economic agents alike and determines the terms of exchange among citizens and between them and government officials. This implies that the capacity of an existing governance structure plays a critical role concerning (i) the formation, implementation, and enforcement of economic and social policies as well as development projects; and (ii) private sector development and co-ordination. With respect to problems of initiating, implementing and sustaining government policies, the *political institutions* of a country's governance structure play a dominant role, because they determine how different actors are involved in political processes, what kinds of economic reforms are politically feasible and how the behaviour of individual actors is shaped.

Governance structures are based on four key principles – accountability, participation, predictability and transparency – which are required for the sound management of public resources, an enabling environment for the private sector and a productive partnership between the public and private sectors which does not degrade into closed circles of influence and privilege. Governance provides the overall perspective from which these principles are derived.[20] Capacity building, a term which is often used in combination with governance, refers to the action proposed to achieve these principles (see Table 4.1).[21] Confusing these two terms would imply that operationally capacity-building work in the narrow sense might be interpreted as governance in the broad sense. Thus, each effort at capacity-building would be considered a governance activity implying the danger that policy makers do not take the complexity of a governance structure into account but tend to tackle governance problems in an *ad hoc* manner.

*Table 4.1  Governance and  capacity-building*

| Governance building | Capacity |
| --- | --- |
| Accountability | Public sector management |
| | Public enterprise management and reform |
| | Public financial management |
| | Civil service reform |
| Participation | Participation of beneficiaries and affected groups in projects |
| | Public–private interface |
| | Decentralisation of economic functions and empowerment of local government |
| | Co-operation with NGOs |
| Predictibility | Legal and regulatory reform |
| | Legal framework for private sector development |
| Transparency | Disclosure of information |
| | Stable and clear rules of the game |

Recent studies of the political economy of policy reform show that the complex co-ordination and collective-action problems associated with policy reform can be mitigated by politically-crafted self-enforcing governance structures. These structures change transaction costs, reduce information asymmetries, stabilise expectations, and prompt political authorities promote economic development in a sustainable way.[22] Relatively low political transaction costs are necessary in order to facilitate legislative exchange, to monitor bureaucratic behaviour more effectively, and to improve public sector management and also the interaction of the various branches of government, business representatives and social groups. In another respect, however, a governance structure to be effective needs to increase political transaction costs. This is particularly important in order to prompt policy makers to credibly precommit to abide by the rules of the game and to enhance the incentive compatibility of public policies and economic performance. In order to create credible limits on their own authority, policy makers need to tie their own hands by establishing suitably designed political rules, the revision or transgression of which is associated with high transaction costs. Governance mechanisms which prevent policy makers from acting opportunistically and restrain arbitrary state action include the rule of law, institutional checks and balances through horizontal and vertical separation of powers, an independent judiciary and effective watchdog organisations.[23]

Furthermore, an adequate institutional environment for policy reform needs to provide mechanisms of consensual conflict resolution, enhance political and social stability through transparent rules and processes about how to solve collective problems, and create public trust on the basis of a common sense of legitimate authority.[24] Effective governance structures adequately adjust political transaction costs and mitigate the multiple principal–agent problems which are inherent to policy reform. The existence of multi-principal and multi-task agencies embedded in a multiple-level principal-agent framework imposes severe restrictions on the formulation and implementation of public policies. These constraints, resulting from imperfect and asymmetric information, difficulties in monitoring bureaucratic input and output as well as the activities of private agents, opportunistic behaviour, multiplicity of interests, bounded rationality, and time inconsistency, cause political transaction costs. Instead of imposing additional formal constraints on administrative units, as is often observed in government bureaucracies, effective governance structures need to rely on more sophisticated institutional arrangements – with powerful incentive schemes and screening, signalling and monitoring mechanisms – which imply a fusion of interests of politicians, bureaucrats, business and non-elites.[25] Institutional mechanisms which help improve public sector management may comprise:

- the introduction of hard budget constraints that help delimit the influence of external actors on government expenditures and measure bureaucrats' ability in macroeconomic management;
- meritocratic recruitment and promotion procedures and competitive wages for bureaucrats that can attract more talented individuals and increase integrity and professionalism;
- effective accounting and auditing practices to enhance the financial accountability of policy makers;
- independent personnel agencies which reduce external pressure on appointments and patronage;

- statutory boards partitioning the policy space by assigning single policies to special agencies that help monitor civil servants' performance;
- anti-corruption agencies which reduce bureaucrats' propensity to use their specific information for extra-legal activities; and
- socially connecting an independent bureaucracy through deliberation councils or informal institutions in order to encourage the mutual exchange of information between the public administration and the private sector, enhance the bureaucracy's flexibility, and support a consensual and transparent process of policy formulation.[26]

A governance structure is *effective* if it ensures that policies and projects conducted by governments are properly implemented and enforced and that private businesses can thrive within a given legal and regulatory framework, which is not subject to arbitrary political interference.

From this perspective, effective governance is independent of the basic character of a political system (the regime type), but results from the realisation of a *strong but limited government:* strong in the sense that it is able to precommit itself credibility to policies which are in the interests of its constituency, and to establish an independent bureaucracy capable of implementing and enforcing those policies; limited in the sense that both the government and the public administration are prevented from confiscating private wealth and are held accountable for their activities. By establishing strong but limited governments, institutions can be designed and incentives created which channel the behaviour of political decision makers into those activities which are compatible with sustained transformation and prompt private business to carry out long-term investment and provide the authorities with information that is necessary to make viable policy choices.[27]

## THE NEED FOR STRENGTHENING GOVERNANCE STRUCTURES IN POST-SOCIALIST COUNTRIES

At the onset of transition, stabilisation-cum-adjustment and privatisation policies were undertaken to establish market-orientated economies rapidly in order to solidify transformation, to prevent a potential reversal and to avoid asset stripping state-owned enterprises. What was overlooked or consciously ignored then was that a functioning market economy requires an adequate institutional infrastructure providing market-preserving and market-enhancing incentives to both policy makers and private business. There is broad evidence that in numerous countries insufficient attention and resources were devoted to crafting new institutions and to making policy making more efficient, effective, and accountable. In the light of the alleged dichotomy of states and markets, policy makers, foreign advisers and international organisations advocated a minimalist state and aimed at a drastic reduction in the size and scope of government.[28] A recent United Nations Development Programme (UNDP) report concludes that:

> [T]he 'shrinking state' ... in many parts of the region has contributed to worrying trends in human development, including high rates of poverty, rapidly growing economic and social inequality amounting to socio-economic fragmentation, deterioration in public health and public education, and worrying trends in culture and the long-term health of the environment.[29]

Initially, governance problems were viewed as parts of a secondary reform agenda or expected to be overcome automatically by getting the prices and macroeconomic fundamentals right. The neglect of governance issues may also have been caused by a surge of anti-statism resulting from the demise of the communist state and the policy prescriptions of neoclassical economics. In particular, the Washington consensus – on which most policy recommendations of the Bretton Woods organisations have been based – disregards the question of how state institutions can be effectively reformed in order to help policy makers perform their new roles in a market-orientated environment.

As policy makers, academics, and donor agencies have gradually recognised that systemic transformation is an incremental and continuous process, the need for institution and capacity building is seen as crucial for effective policy formulation and programme implementation. The strengthening of governance structures is now regarded as a *conditio sine qua non* for the consolidation of prior reform achievements and the initiation of further reforms. Meanwhile, most Central and Eastern European countries have made significant progress in changing the nature and the structure of their state apparatuses. This primarily holds for privatisation and the reorientation of those policies which are on the front line of policy reform.[30]

In particular, the transformation process has been strengthened in those countries which have a prospect of acceding to the European Union (EU). Piazolo argues that the credibility of policy reform has been, and will continue to be, enhanced in these countries through institutional reforms.[31] For EU membership will only be granted if the transition countries are able to meet EU standards and norms with respect to the institutional foundation of their economic, legal and political systems. In particular, prospective members need to implement the *acquis communautaire* that includes numerous institutional components which are critical for a functioning market economy. By adopting institutional arrangements that are consistent with EU standards, the governments of these countries tie their own hands and improve their governance structure, so that arbitrary policy changes become less likely. Moreover, the power of vested interests to influence domestic policy making will be reduced and hence the predictability of public policies enhanced. The institutional integration of the Central

European countries has been essentially based on the so-called Europe Agreements, which grant the transition countries associate status in economic and political terms.[32] These Agreements represent the legal basis of the relations between the Central European countries and the EU. They help to enhance the credible commitment to policy reform and to make public policies transparent and predictable, because non-compliance may imply a loss of benefits and postponement or even denial of EU membership.[33] As can be discerned from Table 4.2, to date, most Central and Eastern European countries have achieved substantial progress in institutional reforms concerning the trade and foreign exchange regime, privatisation and the legal system, while the reform progress in areas such as corporate governance, competition policy and financial markets has been modest or diverse. Furthermore, Nunberg found in her cross-country analysis that the restructuring of the core institutions of government has been moderate and reforms have been slow to materialise.[34] Both governments and donor agencies have been hesitant in initiating and supporting programmes aimed at enhancing administrative efficiency and making public–private co-operation and co-ordination more effective.

In contrast to the economic and political progress in CEE, however, Table 4.2 reveals the poor performance of the CIS countries, notably Russia, in which governance-related problems have most severely impeded policy reform. In particular, low capacity and capability of all branches of government have been critical obstacles to progress in most areas of policy reform. The restructuring of the state is still at its very beginning, and reforms have been impeded by a lack of accountability mechanisms and an unstable and non-transparent policy framework.[35] The late 1990s crisis in the Russian Federation, which constituted a considerable setback in economic transition, arose largely from a failure of political institutions (including the inability to collect taxes, to implement administrative and financial sector reform, and to enforce laws). In this respect, the EBRD concluded in 1998:

> [T]hat the way in which markets are liberalised and state enterprises are privatised – that is, the nature of the early transition decisions – can have important implications for the capacity of governments to enforce the rule of law, to promote competition and to regulate effectively. Liberalisation that leaves large profits to be earned from flawed markets and favouritism in privatisation that places industry and finance in the hands of vested interests with powerful political connections can create serious obstacles to further advances in market-oriented reform.[36]

From the beginning of the transition process, Russian authorities have failed to shield policy-making from manipulative and strong pressure groups reflecting the interests of both the old *nomenklatura* and the new oligarchs. These political bottlenecks induced an open flank of policy reform and contributed to the collapse of the financial sector in 1998.

Table 4.2    Progress in institutional change in Central and Eastern Europe and the Commonwealth of independent States (1998)*

| Central and Eastern Europe† | Enterprises | | | Markets and Trade | | | Financial Institutions | | Legal reforms | | Institutional change |
|---|---|---|---|---|---|---|---|---|---|---|---|
| | (1.1) | (1.2) | (1.3) | (2.1) | (2.2) | (2.3) | (3.1) | (3.2) | (4.1) | (4.2) | (5) |
| Albania | 2 | 4 | 2 | 3 | 4 | 2 | 2 | 1.67 | 2 | 2 | 24.67 |
| Bosnia/Herzegovina | 2 | 2 | 1.67 | 3 | 2 | 1 | 2 | 1 | 2 | 1 | 17.67 |
| Bulgaria | 3 | 3 | 2.33 | 3 | 4 | 2 | 2.67 | 2 | 4 | 4 | 30.00 |
| Croatia | 3 | 4.33 | 2.67 | 3 | 4 | 2 | 2.67 | 2.33 | 4 | 3 | 31.00 |
| Czech Republic | 4 | 4.33 | 3 | 3 | 4.33 | 3 | 2.67 | 3 | 4 | 4 | 35.66 |
| Estonia | 4 | 4.33 | 2.67 | 3 | 4 | 2.67 | 3.33 | 3 | 3 | 4 | 34.33 |
| FYROM | 3 | 4 | 2 | 3 | 4 | 1 | 3 | 1.67 | 3 | 4 | 28.67 |
| Hungary | 4 | 4.33 | 3.33 | 3.33 | 4.33 | 3 | 4 | 3.33 | 4 | 4 | 37.65 |
| Latvia | 3 | 4 | 2.67 | 3 | 4 | 2.67 | 2.67 | 2.33 | 3.33 | 2 | 29.67 |
| Lithuania | 3 | 4 | 2.67 | 3 | 4 | 2.33 | 3 | 2.33 | 3 | 3 | 31.33 |
| Poland | 3.33 | 4.33 | 3 | 3.33 | 4.33 | 3 | 3.33 | 3.33 | 4 | 4 | 35.98 |
| Romania | 2.67 | 3.33 | 2 | 3 | 4 | 2 | 2.33 | 2 | 4 | 4 | 29.33 |
| Slovak Republic | 4 | 4.33 | 2.67 | 3 | 4.33 | 3 | 2.67 | 2.33 | 3 | 2 | 31.33 |
| Slovenia | 3.33 | 4.33 | 2.67 | 3 | 4.33 | 2 | 3 | 3 | 3 | 3 | 31.66 |

| Commonwealth of Independent States† | Enterprises | | | Markets and Trade | | | Financial Institutions | | Legal reforms | | Institutional change |
|---|---|---|---|---|---|---|---|---|---|---|---|
| | (1.1) | (1.2) | (1.3) | (2.1) | (2.2) | (2.3) | (3.1) | (3.2) | (4.1) | (4.2) | (5) |
| Armenia | 3 | 3 | 3 | 3 | 4 | 2 | 2.33 | 2 | 4 | 3 | 28.33 |
| Azerbaijan | 2 | 2 | 2 | 3 | 3 | 1 | 2 | 1.67 | 3 | 2 | 22.67 |
| Belarus | 1 | 2 | 1 | 2 | 1 | 2 | 1 | 2 | 3 | 2 | 16.00 |
| Georgia | 3.33 | 4 | 2 | 3 | 4 | 2 | 2.33 | 1 | 3 | 3 | 27.66 |
| Kazakhstan | 3 | 4 | 2 | 3 | 4 | 2 | 2.33 | 2 | 2.33 | 2 | 26.66 |
| Moldova | 3 | 3.33 | 2 | 3 | 4 | 2 | 2.33 | 2 | 4 | 3 | 28.66 |
| Russian Federation | 3.33 | 4 | 3 | 2.67 | 2.33 | 2.33 | 2 | 1.67 | 3.67 | 2 | 26.00 |
| Tajikistan | 2 | 2.33 | 1.67 | 3 | 1 | 1 | 1 | 1 | 1 | 1 | 19.67 |
| Turkmenistan | 1.67 | 2 | 1.67 | 2 | 1 | 1 | 1 | 1 | 1 | 1 | 13.34 |
| Ukraine | 2.33 | 3.33 | 2 | 3 | 2.67 | 2 | | 2 | 2 | 2 | 23.33 |
| Uzbekistan | 2.67 | 3 | 2 | 2 | 1.67 | 2 | 1.67 | 2 | 2.33 | 2 | 21.34 |

*Notes:* * Progress in institutional change is estimated for nine areas and valued on a scale from 1 (little progress) to 5 (standards and performance comparable to advanced industrial countries). The figures in the table represent achieved level in 1998. For legal reforms in Turkmenistan 'na' in European Bank for Reconstruction and Development, *Transition Report* (London 1998) was substituted with '1' (similar to the assessment in European Bank for Reconstruction and Development, *Transition Report* (London 1996). Pluses (+) and minuses (–) for Table 2.2 in EBRD (1998) were transformed into numerical values by adding or subtracting 0.33 from the figures, respectively.

† Large-scale privatisation (1.1); Small-scale privatisation (1.2); Governance and enterprise restructuring (1.3); Price liberalisation (2.1); Trade and foreign exchange system (2.2); Competition policy; Banking reform and interest rate liberalisation (3.1); Securities markets and non-bank financial institutions (3.2); Extensiveness of legal rules (4.1); Effectiveness on investment (4.2); Indicator of institutional change.

*Source:* EBRD (1998) and authors' calculations.

In brief, the most significant governance-related problems which have threatened the success of the transition in CEE and the CIS have resulted from:

- the existence of weak states, the capacity and capability of which have been eroded and which are chronically unable to enforce laws, collect taxes, resist pressure from interest groups, and implement coherent market-orientated reforms;
- a lack of consistent political leadership and credible commitment to policy reform;
- weak local governments and ill-defined central–local government relations;
- widespread corruption resulting from excessive bureaucratic interference and regulations;
- poor and inconsistent public-procurement procedures which are in many instances still based on administrative orders and only partly on market bidding;
- weak supervisory and regulatory structures for the financial sector;
- institution failures due to a contradiction of existing laws, lack of law enforcement, and lack of legal transparency;
- a conflict of formal and informal institutions inducing hysteresis effects;
- resistance to further reform by the winners of the early reform stages, who assumed substantial political power and seek to sustain a partial reform equilibrium;[37]
- an underdeveloped civil society;
- a lack of tradition concerning consultation, and transparent and evenhanded co-operation, with interest groups and other affected groups prior to the introduction of new laws and policies and;
- a lack of experience in explaining the need for, and the rationale of, policy reform to the population at large.

Most of these problems still exist to some degree in all transition countries, but they are more serious the further east one travels and the less likely it is for a particular country to become integrated into the economy of the EU.

The modest and uneven progress in meeting the institutional and structural challenges of the next phase of transition – including the improvement of corporate-governance structures and enterprise restructuring, infrastructure reform, and financial, fiscal and social sector reforms – reflects the lack of an adequate politico-institutional foundation of policy making in the PSCs, which had been shaped by the early transition policies as well as the country-specific legacies inherited from the former socialist regime. To overcome the current impediments to policy reform, a constructive role of governments is required at a time when their capacities are still insufficiently developed and state apparatuses are susceptible to capture by powerful pressure groups. Hence, the unfinished agenda of policy reform in PSCs includes governance-related problems to a significant degree. In particular, institution and capacity building is a pivotal precondition for further stabilisation, structural adjustment and poverty reduction. Major policy lessons implied by these problems include: (i) institutional reforms must not be postponed or delayed if the economic and political gains from liberalisation, stabilisation, and privatisation are to be realised; (ii) the causes of poor public sector performance must be addressed before capacity can be rebuilt; (iii) the effectiveness of institutional reforms depends greatly on how these reforms take into consideration the historical, social, customary and religious factors in a given society; and (iv) almost all transition countries will need continuous technical assistance to support the crafting of public sector institutions, norms and rules for private sector development, and the institutions of civil society.

## GOVERNANCE AND DEVELOPMENT: THE APPROACH OF MULTILATERAL FINANCIAL ORGANISATIONS

Recently, governance has emerged as a *leitmotiv* of numerous bilateral aid programmes and as a pivotal concern of multilateral development agencies. It owes its current relevance to several factors including the misuse of aid funds by recipients, a growing awareness of the growth-impeding effects of corruption, the resurgence of ethnic conflicts in many countries, and the sobering experience with structural adjustment programmes in less-developed countries which have not brought about the expected outcomes. Latterly, the growing focus on governance issues has been given new impetus by the collapse of the totalitarian states in CEE and the CIS and by the popular call for multiparty democracy in Africa and Latin America.

Since numerous PSCs have unstable polities and poor systems of governance and also face severe resource constraints, the major donor agencies may prove to be key players on the politico-economic stage, able to provide considerable assistance and to exert considerable influence. In addressing governance issues, however, external agencies need to go beyond criticising particular economic reform programmes or development projects, questioning the ability of political authorities to govern effectively in the collective interest.[38] Consequently, in practical and operational terms, governance work always touches politically sensitive areas, even if donors seek to confine themselves to the economic and social dimensions of governance because of their inherent political implications.

While some multilateral donors – such as the UNDP – and many bilateral donor agencies, most notably the United States Agency for International Development (USAID), address governance problems in a normative and positive manner and also include political objectives such as democratisation and the improvement of human rights on their governance agendas, most multilateral financial organisations are not allowed to interfere in the sovereignty of the member countries. Nevertheless, the World Bank, the IMF and the EBRD – belonging to the major donor agencies in CEE and the CIS – have all recognised that technical solutions are not sufficient to promote economic growth and development and that governance plays a crucial role in the transition toward open market-orientated economies and for effective policy reforms. They view governance as a means to an end and have begun to give governance issues heightened prominence on their operational agendas – which are now briefly discussed in turn.

**The World Bank**

The World Bank was the first of the multilateral donor agencies that *expressis verbis* gave prominence to governance issues in economic development.[39] Since the beginning of the 1990s, the volume of its governance-related activities has increased substantially. The main geographical focus has been on Africa, Latin America and the Caribbean. Governance work relating to CEE and the CIS, however, is still at an early stage.

The Bank identified three dimensions of governance: (i) the form of the political regime; (ii) the processes by which authority is exercised in the management of a country's economic and social resources; and (iii) the capacity of government to formulate and implement policies and discharge government functions. Concerning its operations, the first dimension is beyond the Bank's mandate.[40] Hence, for the purposes of the Bank's business, governance has been defined as 'the manner in which power is exercised in the management of a country's economic and social resources for development'.[41] The Bank's governance activities concern its lending operations, economic and sector work, research and policy dialogue. Four components of governance have been identified that are relevant for the Bank's work given its mandate and resource constraints. These are public sector management, accountability of public officials, predictability and the legal framework for development, and transparency and information.

Since a functioning government apparatus is perceived to be a key issue of effective development management, the main thrust of governance-related activities has been public sector management including reform of state-owned enterprises, financial management and administrative reform. With respect to enhancing public sector accountability, Bank support has concentrated on fiscal decentralisation, improving auditing and accounting mechanisms, implementing financial management standards, and promoting competition in service delivery and beneficiary participation in project work.

In order to enhance transparency and the flow of information, the Bank has helped improve public financial management, budgeting systems and procurement procedures. The Bank has also organised training programmes for journalists from less-developed countries in order to increase public awareness and to stimulate public debate on policy reform. In the area of legal and regulatory reform, the World Bank has supported member countries, especially economies in transition, in developing a legal framework conducive to private economic activity. Additionally, support for judicial infrastructure and legal training has been provided. Finally, the Bank has started to explore mainstream participatory approaches concerning project design and implementation.

Only recently, the World Bank has begun preparations to conduct national institutional reviews (NIR) in its member countries. The NIR is a new 'product' that is intended to help assess the institutional foundation of policy reform and project work. Its objective is an analysis of key institutions which are critical for effective governance. Based on discussions with, and inputs from, policy makers, legislators, representatives from non-governmental organisations, academia, the media and other organisations, the NIR is supposed to yield a comprehensive assessment of the institutional environment of the respective country, including its political situation. Hence, the NIR should help identify priorities for institutional reform, which are to be incorporated into the country assistance strategy and lending programmes.

**The International Monetary Fund**

Given its mandate, the IMF is, like the World Bank, strictly confined to the economic dimensions of governance.[42] In 1997, the Executive Board promulgated guidelines specifying the Fund's role in governance issues. While suggesting that 'it is legitimate to seek information about the political situation in member countries as an essential element in judging the prospects for policy implementation', these guidelines also adhere to the non-political mandate of the organisation, requiring the Fund's judgements not to be affected 'by the nature of the political regime of a country'.[43] In particular, the guidelines specify that 'the IMF should not act on behalf of a member country in influencing another country's political orientation or behaviour'.[44]

Using a pragmatic, rather than a systematic approach, the IMF seeks to address governance-related problems mainly through policy advice and technical assistance. For the Fund, areas of major concern include capacity building at the Treasury, reform of budget management procedures, accounting and auditing practices, tax and customs administration, economic data management and central bank operations, and also financial sector reform including related legal reforms. By encouraging the liberalisation of the price, exchange and trade systems and the abolition of direct credit allocation, the Fund has sought to assist member countries in establishing institutions which limit *ad hoc* decision making, rent seeking and corruption. Technical assistance projects have been aimed at enhancing member countries' capacity to formulate and implement economic reforms, establishing market-orientated institutions, and increasing the accountability of policy makers. The Fund has also promoted transparency in the public sector, particularly with respect to financial transactions in the central bank and the government budget. It intends to increase its involvement in governance issues through a more extensive treatment in Article IV consultations and a more comprehensive consideration of those governance-related aspects that are within the organisation's mandate and expertise, in its lending activities. Furthermore, the Fund seeks to treat governance issues in all member countries even-handedly and to improve the collaboration with other multilateral donors. From the IMF's perspective, its primary contribution to enhancing governance lies in its support for economic reforms which reduce opportunities for rent seeking and for strengthening institutional and administrative capacity.

Governance-related conditionality in the form of prior actions, structural benchmarks or performance criteria may be attached to policy measures if economic aspects of governance are to have a direct macroeconomic impact. Moreover, financial support could be suspended in the case of weak governance structures that are conceived to have negative macroeconomic implications, threaten the effective implementation of an IMF-supported programme, or facilitate the misuse of funds.[45] Corrective measures to improve governance may be required as a precondition for the resumption of support.[46]

**The European Bank for Reconstruction and Development**

Basically, the EBRD is concerned with both economic and political aspects of governance. The former comprise *inter alia* administrative reform, tax collection and budget management, central–local government relations, legal, regulatory, and financial-sector reform, labour market reform, private property rights and corporate governance. The latter include member countries' commitment to multiparty democracy, pluralism, and human rights. In 1991, the Board of Directors approved procedures which the Bank should adopt in order to implement the political aspects of its mandate.[47] In particular, it was proposed to assess economic and political progress in member countries in respective country strategy papers (CSPs) annually and not on a project-by-project basis. EBRD activities are guided by the CSPs, which contain an assessment of the member countries' political situation. If a country's political orientation is not appropriate or if a country is implementing policies that are inconsistent with the Bank's purpose (that is, the transition to open market-orientated economies, the EBRD can postpone proposed operations, restrict them or suspend the operations altogether. This, however, does not amount to political conditionality attached to any individual project. Besides this punitive measure, the Bank may emphasise political aspects such as the conduct of free elections, the accountability of the executive *vis-à-vis* the legislature and the constituency, the separation of the state and political parties, the rights of free speech and association and also freedom of the press and coalition building in its technical advice and assistance activities.

With respect to administrative and participatory aspects of governance, the Bank has provided technical assistance aimed at strengthening institutional arrangements of the executive and judicial branches of government. It has also promoted public consultation and participation in the preparation of sector-specific projects. Most governance work, however, concerns the economic issues of governance, which are predominantly addressed in the context of sector-specific projects. Conditionality is applied to project lending and has prescribed passing laws on accounting procedures, privatisation of utilities and implementing a market-orientated regulatory framework.

Given the EBRD's mandate, a key feature of its operations is support for the private sector.[48] Operating as both a development and a merchant bank, it provides direct financing for the private sector, enterprise restructuring and privatisation. Its investments also contribute funding for strengthening institutions and realising financial and physical infrastructure projects which support private sector development. Since the Bank's operational purview is microeconomic and most of its clients are private companies or state-owned enterprises which operate in a competitive environment or which are assigned for privatisation, overall policy reform issues, though important side conditions, play a minor role in the Bank's operations. This implies that the EBRD is more concerned with economic aspects of governance relating to private business transactions and less concerned with governance issues relating to overall policy reform.

## A REFLECTION: HOW TO PROMOTE EFFECTIVE GOVERNANCE?

The World Bank claims that it has been involved in promoting effective governance for a long time. This has certainly been true with respect to governance issues related to specific projects.[49] But essentially, governance work has been carried out in an *ad hoc* manner. In the Bank's country assistance strategies, a primary vehicle for the review of the Bank's lending strategy in each country, governance issues have been largely neglected or, if taken into consideration, mainly concerned problems of public sector management.[50]

The Bank, like other international donor agencies, has failed to develop a coherent and consistent approach to key governance issues. To date, it has not provided an analytical and operational concept suitable for devising an overall governance strategy for a particular country. This failure may be attributed to several factors. Firstly, the World Bank's definition of governance is vague and provides only few pointers for analysts or development practitioners as to the nature of governance or the factors affecting its quality. Secondly, the components of effective governance include accountability, transparency, predictability, and also participation. These represent highly abstract concepts, the real world manifestations of which are differentiated, diverse and may partially conflict each other. Neither the World Bank nor the IMF provides sufficient guidance about how to unravel and clarify the broad concepts. This, however, would be necessary to gain a better understanding of how different variants, mechanisms, and degrees of them interact with each other and may be practical and beneficial in different country-specific circumstances.[51] Thirdly, governance work, even if it is confined to its economic dimensions, is always a politically sensitive issue.[52] The World Bank, like the IMF, is neither authorised to interfere in the internal political affairs of a sovereign country nor is it capable of ensuring political stability in member countries. But occasionally it is difficult to draw a distinct boundary between economic conditionality and political interference. For instance, the call for greater transparency and accountability in policy making may implicitly require freedom of the media and free political elections. Therefore, governance work, which is intended to promote economic adjustment and development, turns out to be a difficult balancing act. This political sensitiveness may have prompted the Bank to adopt a rather loose definition of governance and inhibited the organisation in elucidating and specifying its broad and abstract approach. However, the exploration of modes of intervention that are politically feasible, justifiable, and promising is a necessary undertaking if the notion of effective governance is to become a leading and broadly accepted principle in the organisation's operations. Fourthly, as the Bank itself concedes, it lacks adequate expertise in public sector management, institution building and participatory approaches and, one must add, in political science and sociology.[53] This represents a serious impediment to effective handling of the complexity inherent in the governance issue, to suitably addressing governance concerns into the Bank's operations, and to improving the Bank management's understanding of country-specific political, social, cultural, and ethnic side conditions to economic policy making.

The IMF's envisaged approach to governance, which still lacks a proper definition of the term, is restricted to governance-related problems in public resource management and (financial) market regulation. Instead of seeking a theoretical foundation and applying it to national circumstances, the IMF is looking for best practices as a basis for developing new standards to be applied evenly across countries. From the perspective of the IMF role – and given its traditional purview and expertise – economic liberalising plus related institution building is the best way to curb rent seeking, corruption and preferential treatment of privileged elites – and hence to improve governance. The call for leaner and more effective government, the application of neoclassical policy prescriptions, and the even-handed treatment of member countries, however, ignore country-specific circumstances, informal institutions and historical factors.

This neglect may turn out to be counterproductive, because non-economic factors may have a significant impact on the efficacy of policy reforms. If these are neglected, and if future political and social consequences resulting from recommended policy adjustment packages are not taken into account, policy reform may be doomed to failure, especially if existing governance structures are weak. Therefore, international donor organisations need to explore suitable ways to reduce the number of cases in which anticipated reform success evolves into unexpected and expensive failures.

The treatment of the Indonesian crisis of 1997/98 by the IMF is a case in point. Through the imposition of an orthodox austerity approach plus financial sector restructuring, the Fund unintentionally contributed to worsening the crisis. Regardless of whether or not the recommended policies were appropriate from a theoretical point of view, it must be argued that potential country-specific social and political reactions to policy reforms need to be taken into consideration in order to ensure the feasibility of reforms and not to jeopardise political stability.[54] For policy actions not reflecting the views of broad societal groups can precipitate social and political disruptions which seriously interfere with the functioning of the economy.[55] Therefore, both domestic experts in policy making and international organisations need to take the costs of those disruptions into consideration, even if the social and political ramifications may not be explicit parts of their objective functions. From a governance perspective, the application of standard adjustment programmes based on supposedly even-handed policies cannot be effective.

As noted, the Fund's envisaged approach to governance still lacks a proper theoretical basis. Notwithstanding the importance of standards in technical areas such as data dissemination and fiscal and banking codes, macro- and microeconomic policy recommendations need to be tailored to the needs, capacities and capabilities of individual countries. If these requirements cannot be fulfilled by the Fund – be it for a lack of expertise or a restricted mandate of the organisation – then the IMF should consult and co-operate more closely with the regional development banks and other international organisations when it designs adjustment programmes.

The EBRD is the first multilateral financial organisation whose Charter has incorporated political goals. In accordance with its founding agreement, the EBRD is supposed to work only in countries committed to and applying the principles of multiparty democracy, pluralism and market economics. Adherence to these principles is monitored closely and the political situation is regularly reviewed for country strategies. The Bank uses information on the political situation in its member countries as a yardstick to judge countries regarding their eligibility for external assistance. In a recent *Transition Report*, the EBRD states that:

> (t)here remain a number of authoritarian regimes, particularly in Belarus and in most countries of Central Asia, where effective multi-party democracy has not taken root. The experience of transition to date has shown that the reliance of these regimes on manipulation and control undermines sound economic decision-making and prevents an effective response to economic difficulties once they have arisen.[56]

Consequently, in several cases operations have been slowed down or halted. This underscores that the volume of lending is significantly influenced by a country's governance capacity. In none of these countries, however, operations have been suspended.

The EBRD has been most explicit with respect to Belarus. In this case, it distinguishes three scenarios. Given a base case that reflects current political conditions, the Bank would focus its operations on private sector development. In an intermediate case reflecting progress in the political sphere, two public sector projects – the preparatory work on which has been halted – would be reinstated. The high-case scenario requires substantial progress in both overall economic and political reforms. In that case, the Bank would see a viable opportunity to expand its programme. With regard to the Central Asian countries, which do not meet democratic political standards, no public information is available concerning the influence of the political situation on the Bank's future operational programme.[57]

Despite its mandate, however, the EBRD does not actively pursue political changes in its member countries. It has not interpreted its mandate in a proactive way, but rather in a conservative manner. Political reforms appear to be regarded as preconditions for the promotion of state sector projects, but the Bank does not provide significant assistance to improve the overall governance structure of a country. Institutional reforms that are supported mainly focus on the economic dimension of governance, such as legal and regulatory reforms aimed at enhancing the management of a specific sector in the economy. Since most of its operations focus on the micro level and the Bank is not involved in structural adjustment at the state level, no conditionality exists in terms of policy-related lending and basically no prior policy actions are required for financing private sector projects. At the macro-level, governance work is restricted to a policy dialogue at the ministerial level. With respect to reorientating and restructuring the government apparatuses in recipient countries, the Bank is involved in a very limited way, especially focusing on the legal transition.

In sum, a stocktaking of governance work conducted by the multilateral financial organisations draws attention to eight important facts.

1.   The incorporation of governance issues in these organisations' operations is still at its very beginning.
2.   Although donor agencies, particularly the World Bank, have been involved in numerous governance-related activities, their governance work has been largely carried out in an ad hoc manner and does not follow a systematic approach, let alone a consistent and coherent strategy.
3.   The components of governance including accountability, predictability, and transparency represent highly abstract concepts, which are at times used in formalistic and legalistic terms and occasionally in more specific ways.
4.   The importance of government credibility and commitment to policy reform has been essentially neglected as a pivotal precondition for effective economic reforms.
5.   Governance work, to date, has been mainly technical in character (especially with respect to public sector management), that is, it addresses the machinery of the state sector, but not automatically the sources of poor performance.
6.   There is a lack of expertise relating to governance work. If governance issues are to be taken seriously, staff skills need to be upgraded and new skills acquired particularly in the areas of institution building, public sector management, participatory approaches and public–private partnerships.
7.   Governance-related activities are always politically sensitive and may in some cases collide with the international organisations' mandate. The elaboration of a feasible governance agenda represents a balancing act between the consideration of economic necessities and the acknowledgement of political constraints.
8.   While recipient governments remain the primary partners regarding communication negotiation and particular operations, international organisations do have the right to initiate a dialogue with other political, economic and social actors in the country concerned. This

does not call the sovereignty of recipient countries into question, but gives the donor agency some latitude to overcome restrictions by governments. Donors need to intensify and institutionalise such dialogue in order to gather information, to form an independent judgement in deciding on assistance programmes, and to identify the politically feasible and economically effective ingredients of policy reform.

## TOWARDS A NEW KIND OF CONDITIONALITY IN INTERNATIONAL LENDING OPERATIONS?

Today, it is accepted that the politico-institutional environment in a borrowing country plays a major role in shaping the country's economic and social development, the efficacy of policy reform and the effectiveness of external aid. Therefore, it is only reasonable that donor organisations take the issue of sound development management into consideration in their lending decisions. The crucial question, however, is how this ought to be done given the restricted mandate of both the World Bank and the IMF and the political sensitivity of the issue. Should the provision of development assistance be made contingent on political reforms and improving governance structures in recipient countries? Political conditionality – directed at promoting democratic reform and improving human rights – clearly falls outside the mandate of the Bretton Woods organisations. But is there a political or economic rationale for imposing governance-related conditionality, that is, to make programme and project lending conditional on reforms concerning the *economic* dimensions of governance?

Sometimes multilateral organisations can fulfil the function of agencies of restraint by imposing conditionalities that help governments implement economically necessary policies, which are domestically disputed by the political opposition. But conditionality based on key governance issues will be associated with several problems. Rightly or wrongly, it may be interpreted by recipient governments as interference in their internal political affairs or as neoliberal imperialism by the donor agency (which may seek to impose Western-type values hoping to restrain potential competitors).[58] Policies and projects can often be substituted for each other opening channels to evade conditions which are included in programme loans.[59] Conditionality may be accepted reluctantly, but not implemented as desired. Imposed policies may in fact reinforce hierarchical political relationships and hence exclude particular segments of society which are critical for successful development.[60] The impact of informal institutions on the efficacy of policy making, persisting ideologies, social structures and external security threats contribute to the complexity of the governance issue and may affect the quality of a country's governance structure regardless of the nature of the political regime. To date, it is not sufficiently understood what kinds of political and institutional problems are crucial to effective lending operations in a particular country and which are not. Governance-related conditionality is also confronted with a traditional dilemma of external assistance. Loans or grants of whatever form will not yield the desired outcomes unless the recipients are credibly committed to institutional reforms and the implementation of policies that are indispensable for sustained social and economic development. External support has all too often failed to offset a lack of local ownership of policy reforms.[61]

Governance-related conditionality will inevitably represent a balancing act between an economic rationale and political interference. Furthermore, it is extremely difficult to apply even-handed criteria to measure country performance in terms of governance. Landell-Mills and Serageldin argue:

> in practice country situations are never identical. Moreover, significant improvements in some areas may be accompanied by failures in others. The 'acceptable' level of deviance from an ideal remains a subjective matter. Conceptually, it is almost impossible to reduce the complex social, cultural, political, legal, and economic interactions that make up a modern society to a single measure of good governance. [62]

Individual country circumstances make judgmental approaches inescapable. Therefore, a pragmatic, though consistent and coherent, approach to promote governance is highly desirable.

Besides the punitive form of conditionality (a reduction, redirection or suspension of development assistance in the case of non-compliance), there are two positive forms of assistance which provide the opportunity to proceed in this way. These include an increase of external funds to reward efforts at improving governance capacity and specialised forms of support in the form of technical assistance projects and policy dialogue.

In applying the different forms of assistance available to multilateral donors, they would be well advised to distinguish between different categories of governments – not with respect to regime type but regarding their willingness to overcome governance-related obstacles to policy reform and project management. First of all, there are countries whose governments are reform-minded, willing to improve governance structures, and request the donor organisation to provide assistance. Second, a number of countries exist in which (parts of) the government opposes major steps towards governance reform; and, third, there are countries whose governments significantly violate human rights. The feasible governance work by multilateral donors which can be effectively pursued crucially depends on which category a particular country belongs to. While countries belonging to the first may be reasonably responsive to comprehensive reforms of their governance structure, those of the second are not. If the multilateral development agencies choose to pursue governance work regarding these countries, they need to decide in favour of a more gradual, piecemeal approach. Countries belonging to the last group may still be eligible for foreign assistance by multilaterals beyond humanitarian and emergency aid, if they fulfil the economic preconditions required to implement an economic adjustment programme.[63] However, if lending is eliminated for any reason, the only remaining option is to seek to improve the government's understanding of governance issues through a continuing policy dialogue.

In all cases, government ownership is the overarching prerequisite. Even if international donor organisations seek to base their governance work – or possibly emerging governance strategies – on a 'depoliticised' concept, key governance issues will almost always address sensitive political areas of policy reform, at least in the perception of recipient governments. This is the main reason why governance-related adjustment programmes or projects need to be elaborated in co-operation between donors and recipient countries. PSC governments need to take full ownership of broad-scale governance programmes and also single projects, if they relate to critical areas of policy making, for instance, in the case of establishing a national audit office.

In most transition economies, there is an urgent need to clarify priorities and phasing of governance-related policies and projects. Basically, there are two ways to improve the overall governance structure of a country: (a) through a system-wide, frontal big-bang approach or (b) through an incremental, long-term strategy. Given the political sensitivity and the reluctance of government authorities to discuss governance issues openly, the first approach is not feasible in most transition countries, except for those countries which strive for EU membership. In most cases, only an indirect and gradual approach to improve the overall governance structure will be effective and sustainable and also acceptable to governments, so that they can assume ownership of the reform process.

However, experiences in numerous less-developed countries indicate that the gradualist approach in working with specific sectors and institutions and hoping that the change will spread gradually into other areas of the system can be been defeated by systemic ineffectiveness and produce only 'islands of excellence'. There are no blueprints to overcome this dilemma. Appropriate ways of how to proceed will depend on country-specific characteristics. From a conceptual perspective, however, a *focal-point approach* might be appropriate to enhance the overall governance structure gradually in countries whose governments are reluctant to bold envisage reforms or whose informal institutions would be in conflict with an institutional big-bang approach. Focal points can be already existing or newly-created institutions, performing core governance functions. The strengthening of focal points (supported by external assistance) will yield spillover effects to other institutions in the system through their demonstration function or through induced changes in the incentive structures underlying the behaviour of individuals and the activities of agencies. In addition, *umbrella loans on governance* and applying a *systems approach in sector projects* may be useful tools for improving the overall governance structure.

## Focal-point Approach

Strategic entry points to address key governance issues include improving public administration, strengthening mechanisms and institutional arrangements which facilitate the flow of information, improving actual service delivery in order to encourage user feedback and discipline the line ministries, and assuring a minimum of genuine user participation in order to improve implementation. Since, in addition, a sound macroeconomic policy framework and administrative reform represent necessary preconditions of successful policy reform in transition economies, focal points of high priority may include the following.

- Central Bank. Strengthening the domestic banking system is a prerequisite of macroeconomic stability and the efficient allocation of resources, and hence a precondition of effective structural reforms.
- Ministry of Finance (MOF). Strengthening this ministry appears to be useful in order to address the problems of financial management, fiscal decentralisation and centre-local financial relations. Institutional support of the MOF needs to be linked to the establishment of a national audit office.
- National Audit Office. The establishment of a national audit system can effectively change political and bureaucratic behaviour, because ministries and government agencies must consider that their activities will be closely monitored and regularly audited. This requires, however, strong political commitment to improve public sector management through such a system as a professional office that reports not only to the executive branch of government but also to the legislature.
- The core agency responsible for public administration reform and for translating the broad guidelines on administrative reforms into action plans.
- Offices agencies of the executive branch of government at subnational levels. The support of these institutions in selected, well-connected pilot provinces would effectively complement and support the overall public administration reform process through a bottom-up approach and perform a useful demonstration function for other provinces. In this context, it may be desirable to provide provinces and districts with relatively small budgets even before a comprehensive reform of the fiscal system is initiated in order to enhance flexibility and to support creativity of policy making at subnational levels.

- The government agencies which are responsible for the privatisation of state-owned enterprises and for implementing and enforcing anti-monopoly policies.
- Schools and training centres for administration and management. These organisations are critical to provide general training, particularly of senior civil servants including ministers, in public administration and market economics. Inter-sectoral and intra-sectoral training could be conducted in training centres at line ministries.
- Ministry of Education. Since the educational sector is the key sector to improve human resource development, and hence to lay the foundation for effective governance and sustainable development, the ministry or one of its departments should merit focal-point status.

In addition to the foregoing it is possible to specify a number of focul points of secondary priority. These might include the following.

- Economic Research Institutes. Transforming these institutes into independent research organisations with a clear agenda would improve substantially the quality of policy analysis and formulation, macroeconomic development planning and other key socioeconomic tasks relevant for effective policy making.
- Chambers of Commerce. Private sector development is one of the key components of creating an effective governance structure. Besides appropriate legal and regulatory reforms, the effective and transparent representation of private sector interests is essential.
- State agencies responsible for human resource development (HRD). Since these agencies provide the guidelines on HRD and translate them into action plans, their output will have a substantial impact on the socioeconomic development of a country.
- The state body that is in charge of donor co-ordination and the distribution of foreign development assistance. Since numerous economies in transition are heavily dependent on external assistance, this agency is the key counterpart for donors and line ministries with respect to project identification, management, implementation, and monitoring. Improving the co-ordination with line ministries and their offices at subnational levels, strengthening the exchange of information concerning project design, implementation and monitoring ans also staff training in internal procedures and regulations, disbursement procedures and development of an effective reporting system between this agency and line ministries are of utmost importance.

These focal points indicate some of the key organisations which are of critical importance for the effectiveness of the overall governance structure in a transition country. From a governance perspective, it would be most effective to strengthen all of these focal points at the same time in order to take advantage of synergy effects. However, a donor may realise that support of some of them will not fall into the organisation's mandate, that other donors have already taken the lead in one or another area or that the donor's priorities correspond more to one particular point than to another. Since it is extremely important to avoid both a half-hearted approach to reforming a governance structure and also duplication of effort, and since the government needs to assume full ownership of all projects – not least to avoid overfunding of projects and 'project farming' by different ministries and departments – an efficient and transparent co-ordination of governance support programmes among donors and between them and the government is critical to success.

A major problem of the focal-point approach, and external support programmes in general, is to identify the most appropriate local counterparts of the donor agency. The implementation of the World Bank's programmes, for instance, is essentially conducted by sectoral departments, which have as their counterparts the corresponding ministries of the recipient government. This gives rise to two problems: first, in some cases, the objective of policy reform is to abolish these ministries or particular departments therein, which in turn will oppose reforms; second, even if the survival of the relevant client itself is not at stake, the counterpart may be hostile to the proposed policy or project and endeavour to block or slow down its implementation.

These problems are particularly acute if the recipient country has a deeply divided government.[64] In several PSCs, notably in Russia, the government has been formed as a coalition of individuals or political parties who represent sharply different interests, political convictions and loyalties. Governments often include both reformist and anti-reformist forces. The latter usually represent the interests of industrial, agricultural, or military pressure groups which strive to maintain the strongholds of the former communist system or seek to preserve the current partial reform equilibrium that allows them to capture massive rents resulting from a non-competitive market environment. When governments are sharply divided, a bold and coherent reform programme can hardly be implemented, even if reformist forces supply the leaders of government. Often ministries opposed to reform are still able to pursue their own agendas and, hence, anti-reformist policies. In this case, the pursuit of first-best economic reform policies may be counterproductive, because anti-reformist forces may be in charge of making the relevant decisions.[65] Moreover, the existence of a deeply divided government may mean that external financial assistance is channelled precisely to those ministries or agencies which oppose policy reform. Boycko et al. report that in 1994 the World Bank approved a loan on land reform in Russia, the administration of which was assigned to the State Committee on

Land.[66] This body, however, opposed land privatisation and used the loan to impede reform. Multilateral development agencies need to take these political side conditions into account when they design structural adjustment programmes and distinguish between economically efficient and politically feasible measures. Furthermore, external support needs to be strategically targeted towards those focal points which are controlled by reform-minded policy makers.

### Umbrella Loan on Governance

If the donor agency wishes to place more emphasis on its governance work, a governance programme loan may be an appropriate way to proceed in the medium and long terms. In order to involve the recipient country in the programme design actively and ensure full ownership of the envisaged improvements of the governance structure, such a facility should be designed as an *umbrella loan*. That means that the donor, in co-operation with the government, determines only the overall conceptual framework of the loan (for example decentralisation of social services or private sector development). Given this framework, all ministries, but also individual departments, agencies and subnational entities – and possibly non-governmental organisations or private organisations – could participate in competitive bidding for components of the overall funding. They would do so by elaborating and providing ideas, concepts and proposals for projects which they would like to realise under the umbrella. The donor organisation and the government would serve as referees. If such a loan is considered as an appropriate tool, a modest first step would be to provide a pilot facility designed for one specific sector. If successful, the next step could be a cross-sector governance umbrella loan.[67]

### Systems Approach in Sector Projects

A way to improve governance components of sector projects in the short term is to base projects on a *systems approach*, that is, a strategy that addresses all the main interdependent elements related to a specific project which complement one another rather than supporting a single component. If combined with a *process* emphasis, it promises to sustainably improve implementation and monitoring of the project. To be effective, an implementation period divided into several phases will be required. This would ensure continual assessment of impact and effect and make it possible to apply lessons learned during the first phase to activities in subsequent phases.

The conceptual framework presented in this chapter in combination with the available policy tools discussed above represent a roadmap for multilateral donor agencies to address those governance issues which are pivotal for sustained policy reform in PSCs. Given the problems and options associated with the reform of governance structures, the following policy conclusions can be drawn for multilateral development agencies which wish to enhance sound development management in their client countries:

• Anticipate the social and political consequences of programme lending and project aid.
• Ensure that recommended policies are not only economically sound but feasible, that is, that the institutional and political preconditions are fulfilled which are necessary for implementation and enforcement; in particular, this concerns credible government commitment including its willingness to reform, its capability to implement, and the political institutions' suitability to sustain reforms beyond government changes and exogenous shocks.
• Refrain from standardised governance policies and pursue country-specific approaches taking the recipient country's history and social and political conditions into account.
• Make sure that governments assume full ownership of any governance-related programme or project (otherwise the programme will not materialise, blocked by policy makers and bureaucrats, or perceived as an artificial imposition of the Western-style model of development).
• In the case of a divided government, strengthen the parts of government which are committed to policy reform against the government ministries or agencies that oppose reforms.
• Devote a high proportion of external assistance to support human resource development in order to ensure the effective functioning of an improved politico-institutional environment.
• Involve subnational governments in governance programmes by selecting pilot regions eligible for assistance, which could create demonstration effects.
• Encourage consensus-building mechanisms in the recipient country in order to increase the acceptance of reforms and involve segments of civil society in debates about governance reforms.
• Be cautious regarding governance-related conditionality due to political sensitivity and the traditional dilemmas of making conditionality work effectively.
• Replace ham-fisted conditionality imposed on grudging governments with quiet signalling or a premium approach that rewards reform efforts by increasing external assistance.[68]
• Intensify country dialogue on key governance issues at a senior minister or head of government level.

Governance-related constraints are usually inter-related within countries and their nature varies considerably from place to place. Domestic institution building and its external support, therefore, must be strategic. No blueprints or 'how-to' manuals can be offered. Crafting effective governance structures implies a long gestation period and requires continuous fine-tuning and adjustment to changing economic, political, social and international circumstances. The road to effective governance is also mapped out by cultural and historical factors which vary substantially across countries. This is why externally devised standard models for (re)invigorating governance structures, which cannot sufficiently take into consideration the complexity of persisting state–society relations, may yield unanticipated negative effects. Moreover, explicit conditionality may be incompatible with the notion of local ownership of reforms. Hence, one may agree with Martin that effective governance cannot be introduced by external actors. However, one needs to add, there are strong arguments that external assistance will be appropriate and suitable to support the creation of effective governance structures initiated by local policy makers.[69]

## NOTES

1. In this context, PSCs include the economies in transition in Central and Eastern Europe (CEE), the Baltic states and the Commonwealth of Independent States (CIS).
2. This chapter discusses only governance work of multilateral development agencies. The discussion of the merits and drawbacks of governance-related activities of, and political conditionality imposed by, bilateral donors are beyond the scope of this chapter.
3. David K. Leonard, 'Professionalism and African Administration', *IDS Bulletin*, 24, 1 (1993) p. 74.
4. Leila L. Frischtak , 'Governance Capacity and Economic Reform in Developing Countries', World Bank Technical Paper 254, World Bank (Washington DC 1994) p. vii; Michael Bratton and Nicholas van de Walle, 'Toward Governance in Africa: Popular Demands and State Responses', in Goran  Hydén and Michael Bratton (eds), *Governance and Politics in Africa* (Boulder 1992) p. 30; Goran Hydén, 'Governance and the Study of Politics', in Goran Hydén and Michael Bratton (eds), *Governance and Politics in Africa* (Boulder 1992) p. 7.
5. This holds, for example, if the term 'good governance' is supposed to mean promoting sustainable economic and social development, democratisation, participatory development, fostering the enforcement of human rights and improving environmental standards; see, for example, Klaus Leisinger, 'Gouvernanz oder: "Zuhause muß beginnen, was leuchten soll im Vaterland"', in Klaus M. Leisinger and Vittorio Hösle (eds), *Entwicklung mit menschlichem Antlitz. Die Dritte und die Erste Welt im Dialog* (Munich 1995) pp. 114–172.

6. This definition simply creates a new term without providing any new conceptualization. What makes it particularly problematic is the use of the adjective *good*, which reflects only subjective perceptions.

7. See, for example, Pranab Bardhan, 'The Nature of Institutional Impediments to Economic Development', mimeo (Berkeley CA 1995); Paul Streeten, 'Markets and States: Against Minimalism', *World Development* 21, 8 (1993) pp. 1281–1298; Maxim Boycko et al., 'Second-Best Economic Policy for a Divided Government', *European Economic Review*, 40, (1996) pp. 767–74; David Martimort, 'The Multiprinciple Nature of Government', *European Economic Review*, 40 (1996) pp. 673–85.

8. Mette Kjaer, 'Governance – Making It Tangible', paper presented at the 'Good Governance' working group at the EADI Conference (Vienna, 11–14 September 1996).

9. World Bank, *Governance and Development* (Washington DC 1992) p. 1.

10. The following considerations on the conceptual use of the term essentially draw on Frischtak, 'Governance Capacity'.

11. See, for example, Jakob de Haan and Clemens Siermann, 'Luxury or Stimulus? The Impact of Democracy on Economic Growth', mimeo (Groningen 1995).

12. Frischtak, 'Governance Capacity', pp. 12–13.

13. This conception has been particularly influenced by experiences from Sub-Saharan Africa, where artificially imposed political institutions as well as externally imposed standard development strategies were often interpreted as the root cause for the long-lasting crisis of governance and resulting adjustment failures. Regarding the cultural dimensions of governance in an African context, see Denis-Constant Martin, 'The Cultural Dimensions of Governance', *Proceedings of the World Bank Annual Conference on Development Economics 1991* (Washington DC 1992) pp. 325–41.

14. Douglass C. North, 'Institutions, Ideology, and Economic Performance', *Cato Journal*, 11, 3 (1992) and Douglass C. North, 'Some Fundamental Puzzles in Economic History/Development', mimeo, Washington University (St. Louis 1995).

15. See, for example, Uwe Mummert, 'Making Institutions Work: From *de jure* to *de facto* Institutional Reform', paper presented at the IAES conference (Vienna 1999), pp. 17–22; Svetozar Pejovich, 'The Market for Institutions versus Capitalism by Fiat: The Case of Eastern Europe', *Kyklos* 47, 4 (1994), pp. 519–29; Douglass C. North, 'Some Fundamental Puzzles'.

16. Pejovich, 'The Market for Institutions', p. 520.

17. Ibid., p. 522.

18. Ibid., Preconditions for a market for institutions to work effectively comprise a stable and credible legal system, equal protection of all property rights, and the freedom of exchange and law of contract.

19. Max Weber, *Wirtschaft und Gesellschaft. Grundriss der verstehenden Soziologie* (Tübingen 1972).

20. For a discussion of these principles and the corresponding imperatives for institution building, see Hilton L. Root, *Small Countries, Big Lessons. Governance and the Rise of East Asia* (Hong Kong 1996).

21. 'Capacity-building' includes three components: (i) institution building (that is, replacing a less-efficient by a more-efficient set of rules and functions); (ii)

organisational restructuring (that is, the design of organisational forms better suited to the new set of rules and functions); and (iii) human resource development (that is, in particular training). Hence, capacity building is not to be confused with a pure training exercise. Capacity is the ability to perform appropriate tasks effectively, efficiently and sustainably. In turn, capacity building refers to improvements in the ability of public sector organisations, either singly or in cooperation with other organisations, to perform appropriate tasks. Beyond the set of irreducible public sector functions such as establishing law and order and setting the rules of the game for economic and political interaction, appropriate tasks are those defined by necessity, history or situation in specific contexts within a given country. See Merilee S. Grindle and Mary E. Hilderbrand, 'Building Sustainable Capacity in the Public Sector: What Can Be Done?', *Public Administration and Development*, 15 (1995) pp. 441–63. It is to be noted that training without institution building and organisational restructuring will have no sustainable effect, if the existing institutions do not match with the proposed policies. New capacity is needed to help assure the rule of law and open access to public information. But capacity building also includes the need to ensure that diverse social groups are able to get needed information and participate in the making of public policy. It includes the need for vibrant markets and a private sector that operates in partnership with government.

22. See, for example, Jose Edgardo Campos and Hilton L. Root, *The Key to the Asian Miracle: Making Shared Growth Credible* (Washington DC 1996); Yingyi Qian and Barry R. Weingast 'Institutions, State Activism, and Economic Development: A Comparison of State-owned and Township-Village Enterprises in China', in: Masahiko Aoki, Hyung-Ki Kim and Masahiro Okuno-Fujiwara (eds), *The Role of Government in East Asian Economic Development. Comparative Institutional Analysis* (Oxford 1997) pp. 254–75; The World Bank, *World Development Report: The State in a Changing World* (New York 1997).

23. See, Torsten Persson, Gérard Roland and Guido Tabellini, 'Separation of Powers and Political Accountability', *Quarterly Journal of Economics*, CXII., 4 (1997) pp. 9—16; Barry R. Weingast, 'Constitutionsal Governance Structures: The Political Foundations of Secure Markets', *Journal of Institutional and Theoretical Economies*, 149, 1 (1993) pp. 286–311; Avinash Dixit, *The Making of Economic Policy: A Transaction-costs Perspective* (Cambridge MA 1996); Root, *Small Countries.*

24. In this respect, see Stephen Knack and Philip Keefer, 'Does Social Capital Have and Economic Payoff? A Cross-country Investigation', *Quarterly Journal of Economics*, 112., 4 (1997) pp. 1251–88, who find in their cross-country analysis that social capital matters for economic performance. Civic norms and trust are relatively strong in societies with relatively high incomes and equal income distribution, with institutions restraining predatory state action, and with educated, ethnically homogenous populations. They argue that, in countries in which interpersonal trust is relatively low, the provision of formal institutional rules monitoring economic exchange is of particular importance.

25. See James Q. Wilson, *Bureaucracy. What Government Agencies Do and Why They Do it?* (New York 1989).

26. Note, however, that deliberation councils will only be useful if the private sector is sufficiently developed, in order to avoid collusion between the bureaucracy and individual private companies which have assumed monopolistic powers.
27. See Barry R. Weingast, 'The Economic Role of Political Institutions: Market preserving Federalism and Economic Development', *Journal of Law, Economics and Organization* 11, 1 (1995) pp. 286–311, who provides a thorough analysis of the concept of strong but limited government.
28. Paul G. Hare, 'The Distance between Eastern Europe and Brussels: Reform Deficits in Potential Member States', in Horst Siebert (ed.), *Quo Vadis Europe?* (Tübingen 1997) pp. 127–45.
29. United Nations Development Programme, *The Shrinking State. Governance and Sustainable Human Development* (New York 1997) p. 1. This UNDP report provides a comprehensive stocktaking of institutional and political reforms which have been undertaken in the transition countries since the beginning of the 1990s.
30. These policies include prudent fiscal and monetary policies, exchange rate and foreign trade policies as well as measures aimed at the deregulation of factor and goods markets.
31. Daniel Piazolo, 'Economic Growth through the Import of Credibility: The Importance of Institutional Integration for Eastern Europe', mimeo, Kiel Institute of World Economics (Kiel 1998).
32. The Europe Agreements were signed by the EU on the one hand and Bulgaria, the Czech Republic, Estonia, Hungary, Latvia, Lithuania, Poland, Romania, the Slovak Republic, and Slovenia on the other hand.
33. Note, for example, that *inter alia* for political reasons and persisting institutional deficits the Slovak Republic was excluded from the group of countries which are primarily eligible for negotiating EU membership. The Central and Eastern European countries belonging to this group include the Czech Republic, Estonia, Hungary, Poland and Slovenia.
34. Barbara Nunberg, *The State After Communism. Administrative Transitions in Central and Eastern Europe*, World Bank (Washington DC 1999).
35. World Bank, *World Development Report: From Plan to Market* (New York 1996).
36. European Bank for Reconstruction and Development, *Transition Report 1998* (London 1998) pp. iv–v.
37. Regarding this point, see the instructive study by Joel S. Hellman, 'Winners Take All. The Politics of Partial Reform in Postcommunist Transition', *World Politics*, 50 (1998).
38. Pierre Landell-Mills and Ismael Serageldin, 'Governance and the External Factor', *Proceedings of the World Bank Annual Conference on Development Economics 1991* (Washington DC 1992) pp. 303–20.
39. World Bank, *Sub-Saharan Africa: From Crisis to Sustainable Growth: A Long-Term Perspective Study* (Washington DC 1989).
40. Article IV, Section 10 of the organization's Articles of Agreement states that 'the Bank and its officers shall not interfere in the political affairs of any member; nor shall they be influenced in their decisions by the political character of the member or members concerned.' However, the World Bank also indirectly touches on the political dimensions of governance through its policy dialogues with

governments and through its position as chairperson of the Consultative Group meetings between recipient governments and donor agencies.

41. World Bank, *Governance and Development* (Washington DC 1992) p. 1.

42. Article IV, Section 3 of the IMF's Articles of Agreement, for example, reads: '(a) The Fund shall oversee the international monetary system in order to ensure its effective operation, and shall oversee the compliance of each member with its obligations under Section 1 of this Article. (b) In order to fulfill its functions under (a) above, the Fund shall exercise firm surveillance over the exchange rate policies of members, and shall adopt specific principles for the guidance of all members with respect to those policies. Each member shall provide the Fund with the information necessary for such surveillance, and, when requested by the Fund, shall consult with it on the member's exchange rate policies. The principles adopted by the Fund shall be consistent with cooperative arrangements by which members maintain the value of their currencies in relation to the value of the currency or currencies of other members, as well as with other exchange arrangements of a member's choice consistent with the purposes of the Fund and Section 1 of this Article. These principles shall respect the domestic social and political policies of members, and in applying these principles the Fund shall pay due regard to the circumstances of members.'

43. International Monetary Fund, *Good Governance. The IMF's Role* (Washington DC 1997) pp. 4–5.

44. Ibid.

45. In this context, consider Article V, Section 5 of the IMF's Articles of Agreement which states that '(w)henever the Fund is of the opinion that any member is using the general resources of the Fund in a manner contrary to the purposes of the Fund, it shall present to the member a report setting forth the views of the Fund and prescribing a suitable time for reply. After presenting such a report to a member, the Fund may limit the use of its general resources by the member. If no reply to the report is received from the member within the prescribed time, or if the reply received is unsatisfactory, the Fund may continue to limit the member's use of the general resources of the Fund or may, after giving reasonable notice to the member, declare it ineligible to use the general resources of the Fund.'

46. Regarding a recent discussion of the evolution of IMF conditionality, see Harold James, 'From Grandmotherlines to Governance. The Evolution of IMF Conditionality', *Finance and Development*, 35, 4 (1998).

47. European Bank for Reconstruction and Development, *The Political Aspects of the Mandate of the EBRD* (London 1992).

48. According to its Articles of Agreement, at least 60 per cent of the EBRD's financing should be targeted at the private sector. In 1997, private sector commitments accounted for 76 per cent by volume.

49. This essentially relates to the institutional strengthening of, and capacity building at, a particular ministry or agency as one component of a specific project in a particular sector.

50. World Bank, *Governance. The World Bank's Experience* (Washington DC 1994).

51. See Mick Moore, 'Declining to Learn From the East? The World Bank on "Governance and Development"', *IDS Bulletin* 24, 1 (1993), who provides an instructive and comprehensive critique of the World Bank's approach to governance.

52. See Carol Lancaster, 'Governance and Development: The Views from Washington', *IDS Bulletin*, 24, 1 (1993) pp. 9–15.
53. World Bank, *Governance. The World Bank's Experience*.
54. Regarding the role of the IMF in the Indonesian crisis see, for example, Steven Radelet (1998), 'Indonesia's Implosion', Harvard Institute for International Develoment, Internet Website: http://www.hiid.harvard.edu/pub/other/ indimp.pdf (16 April 1999) and Steven Radelet and Jeffrey Sachs (1998), 'The Onset of the East Asian Financial Crisis', Harvard Institute for International Development, Internet Website: http://www.hiid.harvard.edu/pub/other/ eaonset.pdf (16 April 1999). For the most comprehensive list of references concerning the Asian financial and economic crisis, the role of the IMF, and particular country analyses, visit the Asia Crisis Homepage on the Internet created by Nouriel Roubini (1999), 'What Caused Asia's Economic and Currency Crisis and Its Global Contagion?', Internet Website: http://www.stern.nyu.edu/~nroubini/asia/AsiaHomepage.html#introl (16 April 1999).
55. In this context, it should be noted that the IMF has recently begun to improve its dialogue with members of civil society. The information provided by civic organisations is now used by some IMF staff to make an assessment of the political effects of IMF policies. To date, however, the dialogue between the Fund and civil society has been poorly institutionalised, haphazardly sustained and its initiatives have been improvised and reactive. See Jan A. Scholte, 'The IMF Meets Civil Society', *Finance and Development,* 35, 3 (1998).
56. European Bank for Reconstruction and Development, *Transition Report* (London 1998).
57. Regarding country-specific information on the Bank's operations, visit the EBRD's website at http://www.ebrd.com/english/opera/Country/index.htm (16 April 1999).
58. This is a criticism often voiced, for example, by Mahathir Mohamad, Prime Minister of Malaysia.
59. Paul Streeten, 'Governance', in M.G. Quibria and J. Malcolm Dowling (eds), *Current Issues in Economic Development. An Asian Perspective* (Hong Kong 1996) pp. 26–66.
60. Joseph E. Stiglitz, 'Development Based on Participation – A Strategy for Transforming Societies', *Transition. The Newsletter About Reforming Economies*, 9, 6 (December 1998) pp. 1–3.
61. Tony Killick, 'Principals, Agents and the Limitations of BWI Conditionality', World Economy, 19 (1996) pp. 211–29; Peter Nunnenkamp 'What Donors Mean by Good Governance: Heroic Ends, Limited Means, and Traditional Dilemmas of Development Cooperation', *IDS Bulletin*, 26, 2 (1995) pp. 9–16.
62. Landell-Mills and Seregeldin, 'Governance and the External Factor', p. 305.
63. See Mike Stevens and Shiro Gnanaselvam, 'The World Bank and Governance', *IDS Bulletin*, 26. 2 (1995) pp. 97–105.
64. For a detailed analysis of the implications of a divided government for policy reforms in PSCs, see Maxim Boycko, Andrei Shleifer and Robert W. Vishny. *Privatizing Russia* (Cambridge MA 1996).
65. In Russia, for instance, attempts at an economically efficient pre-privatisation restructuring of state-owned enterprises were counterproductive, because sectoral

ministries sought to increase rather than decrease monopoly power and industrial concentration. This called for a rapid mass privatisation programme as a feasible, though theoretically second-best policy, in order to depoliticize the privatization process (see Boycko et al., 'Second-best Economic Policy' and Boycko et al., *Privatizing Russia*).

66. Boycko et al., *Privatizing Russia*.
67. The umbrella concept is related to the notion of the social fund formula as it has been successfully implemented in some Latin American countries. In these cases, donors are less involved in setting priorities, and the spending of aid funds is monitored by a broadly composed supervisory board, which includes domestic parties affected. See Oda van Cranenburgh, 'Increasing State Capacity. What Role for the World Bank?', *IDS Bulletin*, 29, 2 (1998) pp. 75–81. An umbrella loan on governance, as the social fund formula, may support and involve groups in civil society which are substantial parts of a country's social capital and which are all too often excluded groups of society.
68. Regarding the premium approach, see the instructive study by Ulrich Hiemenz, 'Development Strategies and Foreign Aid Policies for Low Income Countries in the 1990s', Kiel Discussion Paper 152, Kiel Institute of World Economics (Kiel 1989).
69. Denis-Constant, Martin, 'The Cultural Dimension of Governance', *Proceedings of the World Bank Annual Conference on Development Economics 1991* (Washington DC 1992).

# 5. International Financial Institutions and Conditionality in Eastern Europe

## David L. Bartlett

### INTRODUCTION

The recent interventions of the International Monetary Fund (IMF) in East Asia, Russia and Brazil have revived old debates over the conditional lending programmes administered by international financial institutions (IFIs). Critics of the IFIs make two basic claims.

First, conditionality gives IFIs undue influence over debtor states. By attaching strict conditions to assistance programmes, the multilateral lending agencies compel financially troubled member states to undertake economic policies that undermine domestic political stability. Such interventions are particularly hazardous in new democracies, whose inchoate representative structures may not withstand the popular unrest generated by the IFIs' harsh economic remedies.

Second, the substantive contents of conditional loans betray the ideological biases of the multilateral lending agencies, which are impervious to the circumstances of developing and transitional economies. The IMF's response to the East Asian financial crisis illustrates this mindset: a preoccupation with macroeconomic austerity to stabilise the region's newly devalued currencies, which imperils recovery and deepens the wealth destruction instigated by the meltdown; an insistence on the resumption of financial sector liberalisation, which helped precipitate the crisis in the first place; and a stubborn resistance to the restoration of capital controls that might preempt future inflows of 'hot' speculative money.[1]

These criticisms of IFI conditionality resonate in Eastern Europe, whose young democracies are presumed to be especially vulnerable to the popular unrest unleashed by austerity programmes and whose transitional economies are even less suited to IMF-style remedies than developing capitalist countries.

I engage these arguments in this chapter, paying special attention to the role of IFI conditionality in the former communist countries. I dismiss the first claim, showing that the Washington lending agencies wield considerably less influence over debtor governments than is commonly imagined. Their impact has been limited even in Eastern Europe, whose small states would appear to be ripe candidates for IFI influence. The course of stabilisation and adjustment policies in the region is chiefly a reflection of the preferences of East European decision makers, whose enthusiasm for orthodox adjustment strategies has sometimes surpassed that of the IFIs themselves. Furthermore, the ability of the former communist states to undertake harsh economic policies belies oft-expressed concerns about the hazards of IMF-style adjustment strategies in new democracies.

I partially accept the second claim concerning the mismatch between the IFIs' standard policy recipe and the needs of debtor countries. Departures from the Washington agencies' neoliberal model may be prudent for some states grappling with rapid and revolutionary changes in the global economy. In particular, the IMF's position on capital liberalisation does not account satisfactorily for the experiences of developing and transitional countries (including several East European states) that have retained capital controls while continuing on a broadly liberalising trajectory.

However, present controversies over capital controls and related issues obscure (i) the shift of much of the IFIs' East European activities away from macroeconomic stabilisation and towards 'second-stage' reforms (for example, legal and institutional development, public sector management, corporate governance), where the efficacy of conditionality is especially limited; (ii) mounting differences between the IMF and the World Bank over programme design, which are turning the 'Washington Consensus' into a myth; and (iii) the increasing visibility of regional organisations (notably the European Union (EU)) whose role in East European development differs substantially from the traditional conditionality practised by the Washington agencies.

I conclude this chapter by discussing the future trajectory of IFI involvement in the East European transition, with special attention to how multilateral and regional agencies are affecting governance structures in the region.

## THE LIMITS OF CONDITIONALITY

Much of the early scholarly work on the IMF and the World Bank was anchored in dependency theory, and viewed the impact of those institutions on member states as both extensive and pernicious.[2]

According to this school, the orthodox adjustment problems favoured by the Washington agencies generated windfalls for international and local capitalists at the expense of rising socioeconomic inequality and declining growth. The IMF, whose influence had waned in the late 1970s as a result of the expansion of alternative sources of finance, enjoyed a resurgence of power in the early 1980s as bank credit dried up and Third World debt crises mounted. In the words of one analyst, the Fund 'became a sort of global capitalist planner ... tightening conditionality and imposing austerity with little concern for political constraints'.[3]

By the mid-1980s, most scholars had dismissed this conception of the Bretton Woods institutions. Several factors undercut the "poverty broker" image of the IFIs. One was the growing recognition, shared even by some proponents of dependency theory, of the central role of member governments in economic adjustment policy. To assign to the Washington agencies primary responsibility for the consequences of adjustment programmes initiated under their sponsorship was to underestimate the capacity of local officials to negotiate the terms of those policies. The influence that the IFIs brought to bear on adjustment policy in developing countries could only be understood in the context of the complex, if not wholly symmetrical, relationship between those institutions and member governments.

Second, the very diminution of the supply of foreign capital which the *dependentistas* cited as evidence of the increased leverage of the Washington agencies actually lessened inducements for developing states to comply with IMF and World Bank conditionality. Whereas the IFIs' 'seal of approval' previously broadened access to commercial bank credit, their capacity to mobilise private capital declined in the 1980s – reducing incentives for member governments to sign politically risky standby agreements.[4]

Finally, principal–agent problems made it difficult for the Washington agencies to enforce the terms of agreements once they were struck. Adverse selection brought the Third World's weakest economies to the fore of the IFIs' lending queue, while asymmetric information fostered moral hazard by enabling debtor states to conceal the data needed to monitor adjustment programmes. The IMF's and the World Bank's restoration of implicit cross-conditionality via the 'new concordat' further weakened oversight by sending mixed signals and allowing debtor governments to play off the conflicting interests of the two organisations.

The uneven record of compliance with conditional lending programmes testified to the IFIs' limited capacity to shape economic policy in member states. Contrary to the expectations of the dependency theorists, time-series data showed that implementation of IMF stabilisation programmes actually diminished in the 1980s. Compliance rates at the end of that decade were particularly unimpressive, despite an abatement of the global economic turmoil that beset debtor states during earlier years. Of 39 IMF programmes undertaken between 1988 and 1990, 72 per cent broke down.[5] During the same period, fulfilment of World Bank Structural Adjustment Loans (SALs) and sectoral adjustment loans (SECALs) was higher, but varied significantly by prior levels of governmental support. Unsurprisingly, compliance with IFI programmes was highest in countries where political leaders had already committed themselves to adjustment policies. Thus, the main effect of IFI involvement was to nudge member governments along the same trajectory they would have taken anyway.[6]

**The Washington Agencies and Eastern Europe**

The dramatic expansion of IFI involvement in Eastern Europe and the Soviet successor states would appear to have heightened possibilities for the Washington agencies to mould economic policy. From the four countries that joined the Bretton Woods institutions before 1989, regional membership reached 25 by 1993. During the early 1990s, the IMF undertook a succession of standby agreements (SBAs) and Extended Fund Facility programmes (EFFs) in the former communist countries. It also introduced the Systemic Transformation Fund (STF), a special fund earmarking concessionary loans for transitional economies. Meanwhile, the World Bank launched a number of SALs and SECALs to support agricultural development, financial sector reform, environmental management and assorted infrastructural projects.[7]

As small, economically weak and geopolitically vulnerable states, the East European countries seemed prima facie cases for IFI domination. But the actual course of developments in the 1990s defied this expectation, as one former communist country after another violated IMF and World Bank conditions. In 1992–93, Bulgaria breached deficit reduction targets and failed to implement an IMF-mandated tax reform, leading Fund officials and local authorities to negotiate a new standby agreement with looser terms in 1994. Romania failed to meet the budget deficit and foreign reserve requirements of its stabilisation programme, prompting the IMF to devise an alternative package blending a conventional standby agreement with a non-conditional STF loan.[8]

Until its 1997 financial crisis, the Czech Republic attained greater success in stabilisation policy than the Balkan states. Yet the main impetus for economic austerity came not from the Washington agencies, but from Czech officials themselves. In 1990, the Klaus government launched an orthodox stabilisation programme more radical than the IMF's standard package, initiating a number of key measures even before signing a formal standby agreement. Having met all the Fund's macroeconomic targets, the Czech authorities declined to draw on the final two tranches of the SBA and decided to prepay their outstanding IMF debt ahead of schedule.[9] Similarly, Poland's 'shock therapy' programme displayed more the imprint of local authorities (notably Finance Minister Leszek Balcerowicz) than of the IFIs. Poland met most of the conditions of its 1990 standby agreement, indeed overshooting the IMF's deficit reduction and current account targets. Subsequently, a centre–right government launched a fiscal stimulus package that caused Poland to breach its deficit targets and prompted the Fund to suspend the country's EFF programme. But IMF officials then softened their negotiating position, agreeing to a new budget deficit ceiling of twice the level specified in the earlier EFF.[10]

As a heavily indebted fledgling democracy, Hungary appeared poorly situated to resist the demands of the Bretton Woods institutions. But developments in the post-communist period confounded these expectations. In 1993, Hungary and the IMF negotiated a new standby agreement, the centrepiece of which was a deficit ceiling designed to arrest the country's ballooning budgetary shortfalls. Hungary's budget deficit for the following year was double the level set in the SBA. But despite the violation of the deficit target, Hungarian negotiators extracted assurances from the Fund that standby funds would remain available. In the words of one well-known analyst, ' … the leverage of these institutions over systemic change in Hungary remained as limited as that in any country on the globe …. Hungary seems to have been predestined for the role of exemplary pupil, but she has surely underperformed relative to such expectations'.[11]

The East European cases not only dispel common depictions of the relationship between the IFIs and small states, but belie concerns often voiced in the early 1990s regarding the perils of IMF-style policies in new democracies. Some countries (for example, Poland) have exhibited high electoral turnover, while others (for example, Bulgaria) have suffered severe economic setbacks. But the region's overall record is impressive, as successor governments have enacted harsh economic policies while continuing on their general trajectory of democratic consolidation. The chief instances of lagging democratisation (Croatia, Serbia, Slovakia) reflected not the political repercussions of IFI-imposed economic austerity but rather the authoritarian tendencies of local leaders who ascended to power on nationalist or exclusory platforms.

**The Uses of Conditionality**

The inability of the Washington agencies to impose their will on the former communist countries of Eastern Europe, together with the ambiguous record of compliance in other regions during earlier periods, underscores the limits of IFI conditionality. But notwithstanding these constraints, conditionality serves useful purposes for both the lending agencies and debtor states. Current criticisms of the Washington agencies – that conditional lending merely exacerbates the moral hazard problem of overlending to insolvent clients – obscure these virtues.[12]

First, specification of performance targets helps to clarify the expectations and concerns of lenders and debtors, thereby lowering the risks of miscommunication, creating a foundation of mutual confidence and facilitating the negotiation of future agreements.

Second, systematic monitoring of term compliance (however imperfect) by external agencies provides local officials with valuable benchmarks to gauge the status of reform policy and check overall economic performance.

Third, conditionality permits the leaders of IFIs to elucidate to shareholders and stakeholders how they are using organisational resources – a critical issue at a time when public and legislative support for the Bretton Woods institutions (particularly in the United States, the biggest shareholder) is waning.

Fourth, formal assent to conditional lending programmes supervised by the IFIs helps member governments signal to international financial markets their commitment to stabilisation and adjustment policies, thereby improving access to (and lowering the cost of) private bank credits and bond financing.

Finally, IFI conditionality raises the economic and political costs of reneging on international loan agreements, thereby strengthening the capacity of debtor governments to resist pressure from opposition groups to water down or abandon adjustment policies. In this way, formal agreements with international donor agencies resonate in the domestic politics of member states in ways that strengthen the hands of pro-market elements.[13] This suggests that the political influence the Washington agencies bring to bear on member states is subtler and more complex than depicted in some of the cruder accounts popularised by the Western press (for example, the 'scapegoat hypothesis').

## SUBSTANTIVE CONTENTS OF CONDITIONAL LOANS

Criticisms of the substantive contents of conditional lending programmes are more compelling. Critics have long indicted the Washington agencies for insensitivity to the particular needs of developing countries, applying to those states remedies more appropriate for mature industrialised economies. The IMF, whose stabilisation model has remained basically unchanged since the agency's founding despite a highly diversified membership and revolutionary changes in the global economy, is especially liable to this charge. While the Fund's programmes have extended into such areas as privatisation and trade reform, its primary mission is still correcting balance-of-payments disequilibria via demand constraints – to the neglect of structural problems in local production and other supply-side issues.[14]

Three key developments in the 1990s heighten the need for the IFIs to create more flexible policy portfolios.

First, the greatly increased volume and velocity of cross-border capital movements threaten developing countries with abrupt, destabilising inflows and outflows of short-term speculative capital. Premature financial liberalisation may aggravate the problem by stimulating domestic competition for depositors, forcing up interest rates, and prompting inexperienced local bankers to finance their lending activities by taking on cheap foreign loans – the foreign exchange risks of which cannot be fully hedged when local capital markets are thin.[15] This is precisely the scenario that occurred in East Asia, where a large build-up of unhedged short-term foreign liabilities precipitated a financial panic and transformed what began as a regional liquidity problem into a full-blown solvency crisis.[16] One of the primary lessons of the East Asian débâcle is that the IFIs should include in their policy portfolios measures that depart from the standard neoliberal model (particularly controls on short-term capital flows and carefully phased financial sector reforms).

Second, the introduction of sophisticated financial products (for example, derivatives, hedge funds) into developing and transitional economies by Western investors seeking higher yields widens the mismatch between international financial flows and domestic regulatory systems in many of these countries. While the proliferation of these instruments is a welcome development in so far as it expands funding opportunities for local companies and promotes the deepening of domestic capital markets (including the hedging capacity needed to lower the risks of borrowing in foreign currencies), it underscores the need for to IFIs to dedicate more resources toward legal and institutional reform and training of local regulators and bankers.

Third, the entrance into the Bretton Woods institutions of the former communist countries – which face the dual challenge of economic development and system transformation – further highlights the need for the Washington agencies to focus greater attention on the legal and regulatory dimensions of adjustment policy. While legal and regulatory reform is well advanced in East Central Europe and the Baltic states (a state of affairs due more to the integrative processes of the European Union than to the efforts of the Washington agencies), the mismatch between domestic institutions and the global financial system is extreme in the Soviet successor states. The special requirements of the transition countries are well recognised in the World Bank, whose most recent reorganisation expanded the resources of a regionally dedicated division (Europe and Central Asia). However, the IMF's mission in the former Soviet Union has not proceeded beyond minor tweaking of the agency's traditional monetary model.[17]

The empirical evidence regarding the use of capital controls – the focus of current debates over the IFIs' responses to crises in emerging markets – strengthens the case for greater policy flexibility on the part of the Washington agencies. Malaysia's imposition of foreign exchange restrictions in September 1998 drew heavy fire from IMF Managing Director Michel Camdessus, whose objections to capital controls were seconded by US Treasury Secretary Robert Rubin. But the panic over Malaysia obscured similar actions in other East Asian countries: both Taiwan (which managed to escape much of the fallout of the regional financial crisis) and Hong Kong (a bastion of free market ideology) introduced capital controls to curb speculation on their currencies.[18] A number of countries in other regions have also used foreign exchange controls. Chile has preserved certain capital controls and thereby averted the currency overvaluation that precipitated the country's financial catastrophe in the early 1980s – while at the same time eluding damage to its reputation as an exemplar of neoliberalism in the capitalist South. The East–Central European countries, which moved quickly towards currency convertibility for current account transactions, have proceeded cautiously in the sphere of capital liberalisation – a policy choice that helped them to weather the contagion effects of the Russian meltdown. It was not until the late 1990s, when accession to the Organisation for Economic Co-operation and Development (OECD) and the convening of negotiations for full EU admission afforded some measure of external support, that Hungary and Poland initiated capital account liberalisation. Significantly, the one East European country that pursued an early course of full currency convertibility – the Czech Republic – is also the one country in the region to suffer a serious foreign exchange crisis. While full capital liberalisation might make sense for countries with wealthy external benefactors able to provide financial backing amid currency crises (for example, Mexico), for most developing and transitional states a more cautious approach is advisable.

Similarly, the empirical evidence on exchange rate regimes reveals no universally applicable policy strategy. Since the collapse of the Bretton Woods system in the early 1970s, the IMF has generally looked askance at state intervention in currency markets, preferring to allow market forces to determine exchange rates. To ensure that member countries maintain competitive exchange rates, the Fund's standby agreements often include floors on foreign exchange reserves that serve to discourage central bank interventions. However, a number of developing countries have departed from this formula. For some years Argentina and Hong Kong have used currency boards, whose pegged exchange rates weathered major regional financial crises. The transition countries have employed a wide array of exchange rate systems, ranging from the currency boards of Estonia and Lithuania to the crawling pegs of Hungary and Poland to the managed floating regimes of the Czech Republic, Latvia and Slovenia.[19] Regional data do not permit definitive judgements about the macroeconomic effects of these various exchange rate systems. Several of the East European countries switched from pegged to flexible rates in the mid-1990s to correct for real currency appreciation that damaged their international trade competitiveness. However, during the same period Estonia and Lithuania retained their currency board regimes without inflicting serious damage to the balance of payments; indeed in 1998 both registered smaller trade deficits than the countries that adopted crawling pegs or floating rates. Moreover, by that time both of those Baltic states achieved inflation rates in the low single digits, casting doubt on the usual assumption of a trade-off between inflation and trade competitiveness in the design of exchange rate systems.[20]

In short, the range of experiences of member governments clearly demonstrates that the IFIs can enlarge the policy repertoires of their conditional lending programmes without abandoning the broader objectives of economic stability and market reform.

### Shifts in Policy Agenda

However, this analysis of IFI conditionality disguises the fact that for many member countries (including most of the former communist states), the policy agenda is shifting away from macroeconomic stabilisation and towards arenas where traditional conditionality is of diminished relevance.

Notwithstanding continuing disputes over the suitability of the IMF's standard model for transition economies, the general record of stabilisation policy in the former communist states is surprisingly good. Several countries – Belarus, Moldova, and of course the Russian Federation – continue to exhibit serious imbalances, while Bulgaria has only recently recovered from its 1997 financial crisis. Elsewhere, the macroeconomic performance indices used by the IMF (inflation rates, budget deficits, current account balances) reveal generally favourable trends. Even several of the Caucasian and Central Asian states have made notable progress in the stabilisation sphere. Most of the transition economies have emerged from the post-communist recession to register robust growth rates.[21] (A notable exception here is the Czech Republic, once the darling of the Washington agencies, now mired in economic stagnation resulting from its flawed mass privatisation programme, financial sector difficulties and delayed industrial restructuring.)

While the task of macroeconomic stabilisation in the former communist countries is far from complete (and further turbulence in global financial markets could well reverse the above-noted gains), structural adjustment – subsuming legal and institutional development, health and education reform, public sector management, corporate governance, environmental cleanup, energy management, financial sector reform, private sector development and other second-stage programmes – is supplanting stabilisation as the top item on the IFIs' Eastest European agenda. The increased salience of structural adjustment issues has elevated the position of the World Bank relative to its sister institution. The bulk of the IMF's liquid resources are now tied down in the huge bailout operations in East Asia, Russia and Brazil, the costliest in that agency's history. The World Bank, which is principally responsible for overseeing structural adjustment programmes, is taking the leading position elsewhere. The divide between the Bretton Woods institutions was palpable at the 1998 IMF–World Bank meeting in Washington, where Bank President James Wolfensohn made repeated references to the human and social dimensions of economic adjustment – comments plainly intended to distance himself from his IMF counterpart Camdessus, whose public remarks dealt almost exclusively with the challenges of stabilisation in the crisis economies.

This reorientation of IFI operations in Eastern Europe and the former Soviet Union towards structural reform presages further diminution of the role of traditional conditionality. In contrast to IMF stabilisation programmes, which rely on a few simple and readily quantifiable targets, monitoring of World Bank-supervised adjustment programmes encounters a variety of constraints: ambiguous performance measures, complex relationships between individual components of adjustment programmes, and long gestation periods between the initiation of reforms and visible results.

**Increased Visibility of Regional Organisations**

The role of IFIs in the post-communist transition is also changing in so far as regional   organisations – the EU and the EBRD – are becoming increasingly involved in Eastern Europe's second-stage reforms. Not only do the goals and organisational structures of these institutions differ markedly from the Washington agencies: they also use quite different methods to support development in the transition countries. For instance, the EU has exerted a decisive impact on legal and institutional reform in East–Central Europe – more powerful indeed than the Bretton Woods institutions – without resort to traditional conditionality. In this case, the pull of eventual full admission to the European Union spurred the governments of associate members (and now accession candidates) to introduce a wide range of domestic reforms aimed at converging towards EU standards. And in contrast to the Washington agencies, which formally (if not in reality) restrict their activities to the economic realm, the European Union explicitly acknowledges its objective of promoting democratisation in the former communist states.

## THE IFIs AND EAST EUROPEAN GOVERNANCE

The direct engagement of the European Union in East European democratisation, together with the World Bank's increased attention to issues indirectly related to democratisation (corruption, public sector management, reform of state institutions, and so on) underscores the critical role of IFIs in governance practices in the former communist countries.

The founding charters of the IMF and the World Bank envisaged them as 'apolitical' organisations dedicated respectively to helping member states rectify short-term macroeconomic disequilibria and supporting long-term economic development.[22] The inclusion in the original membership of many authoritarian states, whose domestic systems would have been compromised by IFI involvement in political matters, reinforced this orientation. The geopolitical interests of the largest shareholder, the United States (which actively supported a number of authoritarian regimes during the Cold War) further militated against the use of the Bretton Woods institutions to promote democratic reforms in developing states.

The 'Third Wave' of democratisation that began in the mid-1970s and the subsequent end of the Cold War transformed the international political context in which the Washington agencies operated, blurring (if not entirely removing) the traditional demarcation between economic and political reforms. The term 'governance' first entered the World Bank's lexicon in the early 1990s. The Bank's public documents treated this word in technocratic terms, conceiving of it as a process limited to improving member states' capacity to manage economic resources.[23] However, the World Bank's increased engagement in complex structural adjustment programmes in the capitalist South and its entry into the transitional East (where disentangling the economic and political dimensions of development was even more difficult) prevented Bank authorities from sustaining the illusion of the organisation's apolitical mandate.

The Bank's World Development Report of 1997, *The State in a Changing World*, clearly signalled the agency's movement into areas previously considered as falling outside its charter.[24] The document carefully skirted the specific issue of democratisation, employing instead a variety of code words and phrases couched within the broad rubric of institutional development: 'bringing the state closer to the people'; 'greater accountability and responsiveness through participation'; 'diversity'; 'voice and representation'. However, the political underpinnings of the Bank's new agenda – and its implications for governance structures and practices in member states – were not lost on readers. The report called for an expansion of the Bank's efforts in four areas.

1.  *Reforming State Institutions.* Matching the state's role in the market to existing state capabilities; expanding existing institutions to take on additional roles; improving state services by devolving responsibility to local entities ('subsidiarity').

2.  *Public Sector Reform.* Bolstering the capacity of public institutions to formulate and execute policy; outsourcing contestable services to private providers and non-governmental organisations (NGOs); subjecting civil servants to greater competition via competitive bidding for public contracts; raising the effectiveness of the civil service via increased compensation and meritocratic recruiting.

3.  *Rule of Law.* Bolstering the credibility and predictability of local laws by establishing an impartial, professionalised, and politically independent judiciary.

4.  *Corruption.* Reducing bribery and rent-seeking by narrowing state officials' discretion for arbitrary action and subjecting them to increased legislative, judicial and public accountability.

The institutional assets the World Bank has dedicated to executing this agenda still fall considerably short of the financial and staffing resources allocated to the Bank's more overtly 'economic' divisions (for example, private sector development). Much of the work so far undertaken in the state development sphere has been limited to working papers, internal research, and the formation of *ad hoc* thematic groups based in Washington. However, an examination of the World Bank's approved projects for the coming fiscal years indicates a growing commitment to public sector management, social sector reform, local political development, and other governance-related operations subsumed under the Bank's broad 'multi-sector' category. Projects scheduled for the Soviet successor states figure prominently on the list: institutional capacity in Armenia, Kazakhstan and Russia; public finance in Georgia and Ukraine; entitlements reform in Moldova and Tajikistan.[25]

The World Bank's increased visibility in these policy spheres illustrates two critical points. First, it suggests further diminution of the efficacy of IFI 'conditionality' traditionally conceived. While some components of the Bank's governance projects are amenable to quantitative measures (level of civil service pay; number of NGOs created; percentage of public services outsourced to private contractors; degree of popular satisfaction with the quality and delivery of those services), most are not. For example, it is difficult to conceive of a simple quantitative indicator for 'institutional capacity', a central element of the Bank's governance agenda. At the same time, for reasons elaborated above the systematic evaluation of international development programmes serves the interests of both donor agencies (whose shareholders and stakeholders demand an accounting of how agency resources are being used) and debtor governments (which require guideposts showing where they stand in policy implementation). Devising new evaluation methods suitable to the IFIs' governance agenda is one of the foremost challenges facing the Washington agencies. To this end, in 1997 the World Bank's Board of Executive Directors approved a 'Strategic Compact' broadening the authority of the Bank's internal auditors to monitor continuing programmes and expanding the use of client surveys to gauge the quality and timeliness of Bank projects.[26]

Second, the IFIs' foray into governance issues raises serious questions concerning the wisdom of maintaining the fiction of their apolitical mission. The World Bank's current anti-corruption programmes well illuminate the problem. Once limited to the publication of monographs by Washington-based research staff, the Bank's operations in the corruption sphere have extended to highly visible activities in client states. For example, in summer 1998 the Bank undertook a study of corruption in Georgia, a notoriously corrupt country even by the standards of a region where corruption is pervasive. The study included surveys of households, business enterprises and public employees to assess the sources, extent and patterns of corruption in Georgia; a workshop to evaluate the findings of the survey; and the publication of a 100-day 'Action Plan' aimed at lowering the incidence of corruption. Among the proposed measures were regulatory reform (notably 'delicensing' legislation aimed at eliminating superfluous and excessive licensing procedures that serve as bribery mechanisms for state bureaucrats), procurement reform (subjecting the procurement practices of public agencies to increased scrutiny and publicity), public sector reform (enforcing retirement standards for civil servants and modernising the judicial system through freedom of information legislation, disciplinary procedures for corrupt and incompetent judges, and licensing of lawyers).[27] While the government of Eduard Shevardnadze formally organised the programme, the World Bank's financial support and policy imprint were unmistakable.

To characterise the Bank's involvement in this and similar projects as 'apolitical' is an obvious absurdity and a misrepresentation of what the agency is actually doing in the former communist countries. A revision of the World Bank's charter to account for its increased responsibility in the governance sphere would not only provide shareholders and stakeholders with a more accurate picture of the Bank's current operations, but also free up organisational resources for governance-related projects. However, any such charter amendment must be undertaken with great care: to give the Bank an unrestricted mandate to pursue governance reforms would pull the agency into the domestic politics of member countries to a degree that would impair its ability to promote long-term institutional and legal reforms – the acid test of which is their sustainability across governmental changes. In this scenario, anti-corruption campaigns and other Bank-supported programmes would be popularly associated with specific administrations, and would thereby be imperilled by the electoral victories of opposition parties threatened by those reforms.

## Regional Organisations and East European Governance

While the Bretton Woods institutions have belatedly and cautiously ventured into the governance arena, regional organisations have made no pretence of their active engagement in the domestic political affairs of current and prospective members. The Council of Europe's human rights provisions have induced a number of East European states (for example, Slovakia, Romania) to enact legislation aimed at protecting freedom of religion and improving minority rights. The European Union has exerted a much broader impact on the region. Since the early 1990s, the European Commission has used several financial facilities (Poland and Hungary: Aid for the Reconstruction of Economies (PHARE); Technical Assistance for the Commonwealth of Independent states (TACIS)) to promote education reform and other sector-specific projects in the transitional countries. More recently, the EU's regional development arm, the European Investment Bank (EIB) (whose operations were previously limited to the current membership) obtained the Commission's authorisation to initiate funding activities in prospective members. To this end, the EIB has established a special 'Pre-Accession Support Fund' dedicated to the five former communist states – the Czech Republic, Estonia, Hungary, Poland, and Slovenia' – included in the first wave of the EU's eastward enlargement.

However, the European Union's greatest impact on Eastern Europe has *not* come through direct financial assistance or IMF-style conditionality. Rather, the pull of entry into the Community locked the former communist states on to a trajectory of convergence towards the EU's political, institutional, and regulatory norms. This process of 'anticipatory adaptation' began in the early 1990s, when the EU signed association agreements with ten East European countries.[28] The immediate effect of those agreements was to lower trade restrictions on most industrial goods and initiate a phased liberalisation of steel and textile products. Their broader import was to compel associate member governments to enact a wide range of legislative reforms aimed at preparing for eventual full admission to the EU – despite the fact that the association agreements conveyed to the East European states no automatic right to accession and offered them no timetable for doing so. For sceptics of regional integration, the vague language on accession suggested that Eastern Europe might reside in the semi-permanent limbo of the EU's halfway house, *à la* Turkey.

The political dynamic of regional integration changed dramatically at the December 1997 summit in Luxembourg, when the EU heads of state (following the Commission's call for eastward enlargement in its 'Agenda 2000') invited the 'East European Five' to begin negotiations for full admission. Since the formal accession process began, the fast-track countries have enacted a wide range of measures to comply with the EU's *acquis communautaire*: financial regulation, accounting standards, intellectual property rights, anti-trust law, health and safety standards, environmental protection, judicial reform, public procurement practices, and administrative capacity. Meanwhile, the launching of the European Monetary Union (EMU) in January 1999 has spurred the East European accession candidates to begin preparatory reforms of their foreign exchange systems, despite the fact that few expect those countries formally to enter the EMU until mid- or late-decade.

Of course, EU enlargement has exerted a major impact on governance arrangements in other regions. For instance, in the early 1990s the European Free Trade Association (EFTA) countries that had pending applications for EU membership also modified their domestic institutions in preparation for accession. But Sweden, Austria and Finland were already developed market economies and constitutional democracies, which meant that the local state authorities needed only to reform existing structures to meet EU standards. By contrast, the new East European democracies had to build much of their legal and regulatory systems from scratch. To this end, the governments of the Visegrád countries set up special procedures to ensure that all new legislation conformed to EU law.[29]

The institutional *tabula rasa* of the former communist countries has thus enabled the EU to mould East European governance structures to a degree far surpassing the Washington agencies, whose conditional lending programmes often do little more than reinforce the predisposition of pro-market policy makers in member governments. While the EU has supplied technical and financial assistance to support governance-related reforms in Eastern Europe, its clout derives primarily from the mere lure of full membership, which induces regional authorities unilaterally and voluntarily to configure their domestic institutions along Western lines. Among other things, this underscores the profound asymmetry of power and interests between the East European candidate countries and the European Union – what is driving the integration process is the former's eagerness to get in, rather than the latter's importuning of them to join.

Further demonstrating the potency of regional integration as a reform mechanism in the former communist states is the fact that the East European governments are adopting EU-type governance structures despite continued uncertainty over when (and even if) accession will actually occur – an uncertainty deepened by the electoral defeat of Helmut Kohl (the EU's most ardent proponent of eastward enlargement) in autumn 1998 and the mass resignation of the EU Commission in spring 1999. Reminiscent of the Queen's chess game in 'Alice in Wonderland', the EU has repeatedly moved the target for eastward enlargement; but this has not deterred post-communist governments from proceeding as if the target were within grasp. The pull of EU integration is affecting governance structures even in East European countries left out of the first wave of enlargement (Bulgaria, Latvia, Lithuania, Romania, Slovakia) as well as some countries of the Balkan peninsula and the newly independent states that have no serious prospects of ever being admitted as fully-fledged members. For these countries, the fear of being left behind the fast-track states serves to nudge regional governments towards the EU's governance norms, despite their understanding that formal accession may never happen.

## CONCLUSION

The EU's direct engagement in legal, political, and regulatory reform in Eastern Europe together with the World Bank's cautious movement into governance-related projects suggest a recasting of the IFIs' broader role in transitional economies.

A division of labour of sorts is emerging between multilateral and regional institutions in their East European operations. While the World Bank is still active in the Visegrád countries (for example, educational and pension reform in Hungary; municipal infrastructure and urban development in Poland), those states and the other accession candidates are falling increasingly under the purview of the European Union. This demarcation of spheres will sharpen as the World Bank's remaining projects in East–Central Europe are wound up and the fast-track countries move closer into the EU's fold. However, both the Washington agencies and regional organisations (the EU as well as the EBRD and the Asian Development Bank) remain heavily engaged in the Soviet successor states, a situation that has generated considerable overlap in those institutions' developmental projects.

Naturally, the differing institutional structures, organisational cultures, and operational missions of these agencies prevent fully-fledged integration of their activities in Russia and the newly independent states. However, closer collaboration between the Washington institutions and regional organisations would advance their own interests as well as their client countries' needs by minimising redundancy, creating a more efficient utilisation of institutional assets, and promoting exchange of agency-specific expertise.

## NOTES

1. For a trenchant critique of IMF policy in East Asia, see Steven Radelet and Jeffrey Sachs, 'The Onset of the East Asian Financial Crisis', Harvard Institute for International Development, Internet Website: http://www.hiid.harvard.edu/pub/other/indimp.pdf, visited April 1999 (Cambridge MA 1998); Radelet and Sachs, 'The East Asian Financial Crisis: Diagnosis, Remedies, Prospects', Harvard Institute for International Development, Internet Website http://www.hiid.harvard.edu/pub/other/eaonset.pdf, visited april 1999 (Cambridge MA 1998).
2. Examples of this literature are Martin Honeywell, *The Poverty Brokers: The IMF and Latin America* (London 1983) and Cheryl Payer, *The Debt Trap: The IMF and the Third World* (New York 1974).
3. Manuel Pastor, Jr., 'Latin America, the Debt Crisis, and the International Monetary Fund', in Jeffrey Frieden and David Lake (eds), *International Political Economy: Perspectives on Global Power and Wealth* (New York 1991) p. 328.
4. Miles Kahler, 'External Influence, Conditionality, and the Politics of Adjustment', in Stephan Haggard and Robert Kaufmann (eds), *The Politics of Economic Adjustment* (Princeton 1992) pp. 104–5.
5. Graham Bird, 'The International Monetary Fund and Developing Countries: A Review of the Evidence and Policy Options', *International Organization*, 50, 3 (Summer 1996) p. 494.
6. Vittorio Corbo and Stanley Fischer, 'Adjustment Programs and Bank Support: Rationale and Main Results', Policy, Research, and External Affairs Working Papers, Country Economics Department of the World Bank (January 1991) pp. 28–9; Stephan Haggard, 'The Politics of Adjustment: Lessons from the IMF's Extended Fund Facility', in Miles Kahler (ed.), *The Politics of International Debt* (Ithaca 1986) pp. 157–8; Paul Mosley, Jane Herrigan and John Toye, *Aid and Power: The World Bank and Policy-Based Lending* (London 1991) p. 39; Jacques Polak, *The Changing Nature of IMF Conditionality*, Essays in International Finance (Princeton 1991) pp. 43–4; Karen Remmer, 'The Politics of Economic Stabilization: IMF Standby Programs in Latin America, 1954–1984', *Comparative Politics*, 19, 1 (1986) pp. 1–24.
7. Markus Rodlauer, 'The Experience with IMF-Supported Reform Programs in Central and Eastern Europe', *Journal of Comparative Economics*, 20, 1 (1995) pp. 109–11; Christine Wallich, 'What's Right and What's Wrong with World Bank Involvement in Eastern Europe', *Journal of Comparative Economics*, 20, 1 (1995) pp. 59–81.

8. Salvatore Zecchini, 'The Role of International Financial Institutions in the Transition Process', *Journal of Comparative Economics*, 20, 1 (1995) pp. 128–30.

9. Zdenek Drábek, 'IMF and IBRD Policies in the Former Czechoslovakia', *Journal of Comparative Economics*, 20, 2 (1995) pp. 236–41, 261–62.

10. James Bjork, 'The Uses of Conditionality: Poland and the IMF', *East European Quarterly*, 39, 1 (1995) pp. 94–112; Stanislaw Gomulka, 'The IMF-supported Programs of Poland and Russia, 1990–1994: Principles, Errors, and Results', *Journal of Comparative Economics*, 20, 3 (1995) pp. 334–9.

11. László Csaba, 'Hungary and the IMF: The Experience of Cordial Discord', *Journal of Comparative Economics*, 20, 2 (1995) p. 212.

12. See, for example, Allen Meltzer, 'Asian Problems and the IMF', *Cato Journal*, 17, 3 (1998) pp. 267–74.

13. See Robert Putnam, 'Diplomacy and World Politics: The Logic of Two-level Games', *International Organization*, 42, 3 (1988) pp. 427–61.

14. Bird, 'The International Monetary Fund and Developing Countries', pp. 490–92, 502–3.

15. Marcel Cassard and David Folkerts-Landau, 'Sovereign Debt: Managing the Risks', *Finance and Development* (1997).

16. Barry Bosworth, 'The Asian Financial Crisis', *The Brookings Review*, 16, 3 (1998) pp. 6–9; Jeffrey Sachs, 'International Economics: Unlocking the Mysteries of Globalization', *Foreign Policy* (Spring 1998) pp. 97–111.

17. The following assertion by Jacques Polak, the founding father of the IMF model, well illustrates this perspective: ''The exceptional situation in these countries may be expected to subside as and when inflation comes down and the exchange rate stabilizes at something closer to an equilibrium level. In that new situation, the concerns about inflation may to some extent have abated, but concerns about the payments position can no longer be safely discarded. Increasingly, then, the CIS countries will find themselves in the position where the prescription offered by the simple version of the monetary model suffices'. Jacques Polak, 'The IMF Monetary Model: A Hardy Perennial', *Finance and Development* (December 1997).

18. Robert Wade, 'The Coming Fight Over Capital Controls', *Foreign Policy* (Winter 1998–99) pp. 48–9.

19. Padma Desai, 'Macroeconomic Fragility and Exchange Rate Vulnerability: A Cautionary Record of Transition Economies', *Journal of Comparative Economics*, 26, 4 (1998) pp. 623–7.

20. Monthly Update of Statistics, *Business Central Europe* (March 1999) p. 57.

21. See 'Selected World Development Indicators' in the World Bank's *World Development Report 1998/99* (New York 1999) pp. 186–232.

22. To illustrate: Article III, Section 5(b) of the World Bank requires that the Bank's activities must be undertaken 'without regard to political or other non-economic influences or considerations'.

23. Michelle Miller-Adams, 'The World Bank in the 1990s: Understanding Institutional Change', Paper presented at the Annual Meeting of the American Political Science Association (San Francisco, August 29–September 1 1996) p. 14.

24. World Bank, *World Development Report 1997: The State in a Changing World* (New York 1997).
25. 'Summaries of Projects Approved in Fiscal 1998', *World Bank Annual Report 1998* (Washington DC 1998), pp. 115–7.
26. 'The Strategic Compact: Progress and Challenges', *World Bank Annual Report 1998*, pp. 2–3.
27. 'Coordinating Reforms in the Public Sector: Improving Performance and Combating Corruption', Briefing Notes on a Workshop Organized by the Government of Georgia with the Assistance of the World Bank (June 1998).
28. This term was coined by Stephan Haggard et al., 'Integrating the Two Halves of Europe: Theories of Interests, Bargaining, and Institutions', in Robert Keohane et al., *After the Cold War: International Institutions and State Strategies in Europe, 1989–1991* (Cambridge MA 1993) pp. 182, 188.
29. Kalypso Nicolaidis, 'East European Trade in the Aftermath of 1989: Did International Institutions Matter?', in Keohane et al. (eds), *After the Cold War*, pp. 235–9.

# 6. Transformation in the Czech and Slovak Republics: Elite Receptions and Responses

## Karen Henderson

### INTRODUCTION

The Czech and Slovak Republics are an interesting case in comparing post-communist transformations, as they had almost identical political and economic institutions at the end of the communist period, but then diverged as radically different political and economic agendas took hold in the two republics of the federal state, leading to division into independent states at the end of 1992.

Numerous explanations have been advanced for the division of Czechoslovakia, and the apparent divergence in developments after 1992. One emphasises the differences between Czech and Slovak society which resulted from the timing of modernisation processes in the two parts of the country, and points out that Slovakia modernised both very rapidly and within the restrictive framework of communist structures, while the Czech Republic was already one of the most modern societies in Europe in the interwar period.[1] Another concentrates on differences in the national composition and national identity of the two new states, which left Slovakia grappling with ethnic heterogeneity and new statehood, the response to which was a state based on ethnic nationalism, while the Czech Republic was both ethnically homogenous and accustomed to an independent statehood, which led to a civic concept of nationalism more conducive to democracy.[2] Finally, differences in political culture have been highlighted, whereby it is noted that Slovakia had been marked by a patrimonial form of communism, based on personalised politics, and was therefore doomed to a 'Balkan' pattern of development, whereas the Czech Republic had been characterised by bureaucratic communism which was more conducive to the establishment of rule by law and a 'return to Europe'.[3] The notion that there were fundamental differences in the underlying structures of the two states appeared to be confirmed by the débâcle of July 1997, when Slovakia was formally 'decoupled' from the other states of the Visegrád Four (the Czech Republic, Hungary and Poland). It was neither invited to join North Atlantic Treaty Organisation (NATO) in the first wave of eastward enlargement, nor recommended by the European Commission for commencing negotiations on accession to the European Union (EU).[4]

However, even in July 1997 close observation of Slovak political developments indicated that the 'Mečiar era' was probably destined to end with the parliamentary elections of September 1998, since Vladimír Mečiar's popularity had been declining slowly but surely since a high point in spring 1991 when he was first ousted from the office of Slovak prime minister. The new government installed at the end of October 1998 heralded an almost total reversal of Slovak domestic, economic and foreign policy, and early NATO and EU membership again appeared to be a realistic proposition, supported by the country's Visegrád neighbours. This suggested that the differences between the Czech Republic and Slovakia were not, in fact, as fundamental as originally assumed.

There has also been a certain coincidence in the timing of political and economic shifts in the Czech Republic and Slovakia in the second half of the 1990s in general, which strengthens the impression that the two states are reconverging. The image of the Czech Republic as the model post-communist state in terms of economic reform and democratic society – which in the mid-1990s was often presented in a form just as exaggerated as the notion of an authoritarian, balkanising Slovakia – has been partly eroded since 1997. Economically, the 'Czech miracle' was shown to be partly illusory by the economic downturn from mid-1997 onwards, and the fact that the Czech Republic still has some fundamental problems to be faced to some extent parallels the economic crisis with which the Dzurinda government has had to cope in Slovakia. Politically, the Klaus era in the Czech Republic ended in 1997 and 1998, albeit less slowly and dramatically than the Mečiar era in 1998. Continuing popularity among a section of voters indicated that neither of the architects of Czechoslovak separation was an entirely spent force, as each became leader of the main opposition party in their respective country, and the affinity between them was highlighted when Vacláv Klaus declared his support for Mečiar prior to the second round of the Slovak presidential elections in May 1999. The 'government count' is also similar in both states. The Slovak parliament elected in June 1992 changed its government in March 1994 and held early elections in September 1994, but the next parliament went to full term as the third Mečiar government survived for four years. In the Czech Republic, it was the other way round. The 1992 Czech parliament lasted for a full term four-year term, but the parliament elected in 1996 changed its government at the end of 1997 and held early elections in June 1998. In early 1999, both had relatively new governments:

one (the Czech) was one-party, but a minority government; the other (the Slovak) was a broad coalition, but with a constitutional majority of over 60 per cent of deputies.[5]

These developments, together with more recent analyses of Czech and Slovak political views, suggest that the political cultures of the two states may not be as fundamentally different as some have assumed. Recent comparative research has concluded that Czechs and Slovaks are almost identical if you control for individuals' objective economic situation and church attendance.[6] Multinational surveys also frequently indicate that, while there are differences between Czechs and Slovaks, they none the less remain more similar to each other than to anyone else.[7] This inclines towards the interpretation that divergences in the development of the two states in the mid-1990s may have been primarily the result of the alignment of elite agendas, rather than differences in society at large.[8] Similarly, the division of Czechoslovakia itself can be viewed as the failure of consensus or consociational democracy, determined by the fact that the preconditions for its existence were not present.[9] Elite co-operation is essential to consensus politics, and the lack of it led to Czechoslovakia's demise.

Consequently, the emergence of the post-communist political elites in both parts of the former Czechoslovakia is particularly important in understanding both the progress of post-communist transformation in general, and elite responses to the international dimension of transformation. Furthermore, it is elite politics, and its ability both to guide and to respond to public opinion, which will help determine the two countries' futures.

## ELITE AGENDAS IN THE CZECH AND SLOVAK REPUBLICS

It was in the June 1990 Czechoslovak elections that the 'Return to Europe' first became a prominent theme in the post-communist world. It is, therefore, perhaps ironic that Czech and Slovak political elites spent so much time during their first three years of freedom regulating their relationships with each other, rather than making concerted, unified efforts to fulfil the goal of integration, or, as it was more accurately seen, reintegration into Europe. The division of the country was generally viewed as likely to promote the Czechs' chances of early EU integration, while disadvantaging Slovakia, whose chances of market success were seen as much slimmer than those of the traditionally more advanced Czech economy.[10] In the event, the effect of the underlying, structural difficulties of the Slovak economy proved to be very much less than anticipated in the international community – to the point where it could validly be suggested that Slovakia had suffered from an inaccurate 'bad image' abroad – and it was solely political developments after Slovak independence which led to its exclusion from European integration processes in July 1997.

The fact that the political behaviour of one Slovak government in the mid-1990s was enough to exclude Slovakia from the first round of NATO enlargement is a further indication of the fact that the apparent divergence of Czech and Slovak transformation processes in the mid-1990s may be attributable to the behaviour of the political elites. Yet elite alignments were affected by the foci of the transformation process, which had a deeper public resonance.

The most convincing explanatory structure for the linkage between elite and popular agendas is provided if post-communist states are said to be undergoing a 'triple transition'.[11] This points out that such states have to engage simultaneously in 'economy-building, polity-building and nation-building'.[12] These also correspond to the different levels of political decision making. The most fundamental level relates to decisions about identity, citizenship and the boundaries of the nation-state, which last for centuries; the second level determines constitutional rules, which normally last for decades; and the third level – 'the "normal politics" of allocation' – comprises laws which may last for only a few years.[13]

A notable difference between Czech and Slovak politics in the early and mid-1990s was that Czech politics concentrated heavily on the economic dimension of political contestation, on everyday politics. This was clearly reflected in the party system, which was marked by a left–right economic divide.[14] Even as Czech commentators dramatised the economic problems of summer 1997 and the ensuing two changes of government which took place within the next year – leading after the June 1998 elections to the formation of a far from secure minority Social Democratic government – to an outside observer the country did not appear to be sinking into an instability likely to endanger its democratic system. It was merely facing the travails which dominate the headlines in most established democracies. Changes of government and the need to face up to harsh economic decisions are the lifeblood of democratic politics.

Slovakia, on the other hand, was confronted by polarisation on every level of political decision making, and all three levels were intertwined in a complex and sometimes untransparent fashion. From the time when the unemployment rate began to rise far more sharply in Slovakia than in the Czech Republic at the beginning of the 1990s, economic issues and the attendant policy-making options became inextricably linked to Slovak relations with Prague, and the need for greater Slovak sovereignty.[15] The issue of nation building became even more prominent from 1993 onwards, when the newly independent country had to establish its symbols of statehood. Whereas Czechs slipped easily into their new role as the sole titular nation of their state and were little troubled by defining their own identity, the very meaning of being Slovak was contested. When Slovaks looked back into their own history, they could not even agree on who were the heroes and who the villains.[16] The political rules of the democratic game were also in dispute; this was noticeable from the beginning of Slovakia's independence, as the constitution which emerged during the dry heat of August 1992 was identified with one part of the political spectrum, namely the new (second) Mečiar government which had overseen its drafting. The conflict over political rules of the game was summarised by the European Commission's damning criticism that the country suffered from unsatisfactory 'stability of institutions'.[17] This was most notable in the growing hostility between prime minister and parliamentary majority on the one hand and president on the other which emerged from 1993 onwards, and in the fact that the means of choosing the president, and his constitutional powers, were by 1997 a major subject of discussion.[18] Finally, everyday politics and the distribution of economic ownership and power were drawn into the political contest. Privatisation policy, for example, altered radically with each change of government. It also became intertwined with questions of national self-assertion, as the third Mečiar government preferred direct sale to Slovak buyers over attempts to attract foreign investors. Slovakia was to have the 'stratum of rich people', as Mečiar famously termed it, which it had always lacked in the past.

As a consequence of all the above factors, it may be argued that the divergent political agendas established by the elites in the Czech and Slovak Republics played a role in the division of Czechoslovakia. The dissolution of the federation was determined by the fact that, within the two halves of the state, elites were conducting entirely different political struggles with one another.[19] It was impossible to integrate the multilevel debate of the Slovak Republic with the largely economic agenda of the Czech Republic.

Once independent states were formed, it became clear that the republics had very different party formations which corresponded to the divergent agendas. Just as the Czech Republic has a party system dominated by the left–right cleavage which reflects the major preoccupation with economic issues in domestic politics, so the Slovak Republic in the 1990s developed a party system of a type largely unfamiliar in Western Europe, which reflected the multilevel contestation of politics. This corresponds with the analysis of Elster, Offe and Preuss, which suggests that three different kinds of cleavages exist, corresponding to the different level of politics: socioeconomic cleavages, based on interest; political cleavages, based on ideology; and cultural cleavages, based on identity.[20] It is the conflicts of interest which are most amenable to solution by compromise, since the protagonists acknowledge the legitimacy of opponents' demands, if not their correctness. Ideological cleavages, on the other hand, suppose that opponents are hostile to 'democracy' – whatever that might mean – and are therefore not legitimate participants in the democratic game. Cultural cleavages, furthermore, may lead to one side of the political spectrum assuming that some of its political opponents are not loyal to the state and therefore not legitimate actors in its political debate – either because they are ethnically non-Slovak, or because they are 'bad Slovaks', unduly influenced by ethnic minorities or foreign powers.

These cleavages manifest themselves in the Slovak party system of the late 1990s. The protagonists across the cultural, or identity, divide are the Party of the Hungarian Coalition (SMK) on the one side, and the Slovak National Party (SNS), and to some extent the Movement for a Democratic Slovakia (HZDS) on the other. The SNS, since 1994, has not permitted membership of Slovak citizens who are not of the (ethnic) Slovak nation, and therefore excludes Slovak Hungarians from its political field of vision, other than as 'the enemy'. Divided by ideology, and prone to describe their opponents as violating democratic principles, were the HZDS on the one hand and the Slovak parties of the government coalition formed in October 1998 – the Slovak Democratic Coalition (SDK), Party of Civic Understanding (SOP) and the Party of the Democratic Left (SD) – on the other.[21] Both sides in this battle accused the other of not respecting the democratic rules, and both attempted to alter or 'improve' them. Just as the HZDS toyed with the idea of changing the election system, so the SDK-led government changed the constitution to introduce direct election of the president. Finally, there were socioeconomic disputes. Within each side of the opposition/government divide, the left–right divisions became stronger after the 1998 elections. Within the post-election government coalition, the SDK and the SMK are centre–right, and the SOP and the SD are centre–left. Even the bitterest disputes in the coalition – those between the SD and the SMK – have focused on specific issues in everyday politics, and any ethnic dimensions which underlay them were moderated by the fact that both parties considered the other legitimate, democratic discussion partners. Within the opposition, the HZDS showed signs of fracturing internally on socioeconomic issues as it tried to redefine its position in Slovak politics in the wake of its election defeat, and by April 1999 Mečiar had to reemerge into the political limelight and stand as the HZDS's candidate in the presidential elections in order to stem the disintegration of his party.

Against this background, it is ironic that what the international community regarded as a weakness of the new Slovak government installed in October 1998 is actually a strength when one undertakes an overall evaluation of the direction of Slovak politics. The government of four parties, in which a total of ten parties are embedded, had an overall policy direction favourable for European integration, but concerns were expressed about its stability because it contains a broad spectrum of political views on the economic left–right axis. Yet this is 'normal' politics: these are conflicts of interests amenable to resolution by compromise. The more prominent the left–right divide becomes, the nearer Slovak politics is coming to the West European 'standard'.

While attention has so far been paid largely to the political elites, economic transformation in Slovakia was also drawn into the political battle on all three levels – national ownership, rules of the game and regulations. Slovak sociologists have divided elite strategies of transformation and modernisation into different groups: there are internationally accepted strategies, represented by the present government, and also those of the previous government which promote a specifically Slovak path of reaching a market economy.[22] It is the 'Slovak path' which impinges both on questions of identity – what nationality should own Slovak resources – and also on questions of the rules of the game. Privatisation deals as undertaken by the previous government are increasingly coming under attack from the new government on legal grounds: they were not fair. While external observers view the economic policy of the third Mečiar government in the shadow of corruption and 'crony capitalism', it also stemmed from a differing view of the kind of state which Slovaks were attempting to build. The Slovak arguments over economic strategy go beyond arguments over everyday politics.

It should perhaps finally be pointed out that Czech political and economic divides are not as entirely free of contestation on more than one level of politics as might appear from earlier comments. It was the economic difficulties of the Klaus governments which first came into the spotlight as it became increasingly evident that their superficially Western model of market reforms lacked respect for the rule of law. In other words, economic decisions were not being reached merely on the level of everyday politics. Decision-making on the 'rules of the game' had been neglected. Additionally, when Miloš Zeman's Social Democratic government came to power in July 1998, questions of political rule making also became prominent. The minority government was relying for its survival on a rather unusual 'opposition agreement' with the party of former Prime Minister Klaus, the *raison d'être* of which was *not* merely, as formally stated by the participants, to ensure stable government, but also to change the rules of the political game – in this case the electoral system – in a fashion which would permit an alternation of power between two major parties through eliminating smaller rivals. Instead of mediating conflicts of interest between divergent groups in Czech society, an attempt was to be made to exclude them as political actors. They were not attacked in the full-frontal manner with which the Mečiar government had tried to exclude the opposition by designating them enemies of the independent Slovakia: a more subtle argument was employed in which paranoia about government 'instability' was held to be a justifiable 'democratic' reason to eliminate opposition. What was lacking, however, in both the political and economic levels of debate inside the Czech Republic, were issues of nation building. The Czech nation was self-confident in its identity. The racist Republican Party was ejected from parliament by the electorate in the June 1998 elections (thereby, incidentally, giving the lie to the idea that a change in the electoral system was necessary in order to exclude extremists).[23] The only 'anti-system' party that then remained, the largely unreformed Communist Party, was, while notably anti-German, predominantly contesting the basis of the regime and its economic policies.[24]

## DIFFERENCES BETWEEN CZECH AND SLOVAK ELITES

The question which must now be asked is why Czech and Slovak elites developed different agendas. What was the Slovak elites' role, or aim, in contesting all levels of decision making? A number of hypotheses can be suggested to explain the differences between the Czech and Slovak elites.

### Geographic Divide

A first difference is that when the Czech and Slovak elites entered the post-communist era, they were operating in differently structured geographic spaces. In the communist period, Czechoslovakia was a rather asymmetric federation. There was a Communist Party of Czechoslovakia and a Communist Party of Slovakia, but no Czech Communist Party. This situation within the key organ of political power was replicated in many other organisations, with an almost universal pattern whereby national headquarters of Czechoslovak organisations were based in Prague, whereas any central office in Bratislava was responsible for Slovakia only. Even when the powers of the two constituent republics of the federation were increased from 1990 onwards, the political space was distorted by the fact that the same city was used as the Czechoslovak and the Czech capital. Consequently, it is questionable whether Czechoslovakia ever had a truly Czechoslovak elite, and this was one of the problems which made the continuation of the Czech and Slovak Federal Republic so difficult. The Czech and Czechoslovak identities of the Prague-based Czech elites merged, whereas the Slovaks had a Slovak elite based in Bratislava, while Slovaks working at federal ministries in Prague tended to be viewed as 'federal Slovaks', and were often resented by both Czechs and Slovaks.[25]

The Slovak elite was therefore weakened through division. 'Pragocentrism' – a criticism of Czechoslovak policy increasingly heard in Bratislava in the early 1990s – was a genuine problem. More than half of the Slovak elite was left in a provincial capital by asymmetric federalisation, while the allegiance of the 'federal Slovaks' was unclear. The bifurcated nature of the elites in post-communist Czechoslovakia quickly penetrated into party political life. Leading Slovak politicians, including the party leaders, were split between Prague and Bratislava, according to whether they had seats in the Federal Assembly or the Slovak National Council. Leading Czech politicians, however, were far more uniformly to be found in the Federal Assembly.

Against this background, the division of economic power as privatisation proceeded was bound to become a contentious issue. Economic 'Prago-centrism', most palpable for companies with foreign links who needed to access Prague-based ministries and embassies, was disadvantageous to the newly emergent Slovak economic elite.

## Rural–Urban Divide

It may be suggested that the dominating role of Bratislava within Slovakia is less than that of Prague in the Czech Republic. Bratislava expanded rapidly in size after the Second World War, so that fewer members of the elite were born there, and more have rural roots. The leaders of two of the six parties which were represented in the Slovak parliament after the September 1998 elections were the mayors of other Slovak cities.[26] The population as a whole in Slovakia is also more rural than in the Czech Republic: while the last (1991) Czechoslovak census showed that 22 per cent of Czechs lived in cities with more than 100,000 inhabitants, the figure for Slovaks was only 13 per cent.[27] Communications between the two largest Czech cities (Prague and Brno) are far superior to those between Bratislava and Košice, since the two cities lie on major international rail and motorway routes; and they are also nearer in distance terms, in spite of the larger area of the Czech Republic.[28]

## Cosmopolitanism versus Provincialism

A further difference between Czechs and Slovaks is that Czechs as a whole appear to have a greater command of foreign languages than Slovaks, and travel abroad more, while Bratislava, prior to Slovak independence, rotated in a non-international orbit.[29] Slovak data also shows a fairly strong correlation between (a) knowledge of Western languages and travel and (b) citizens' voting intentions.[30] It might be suggested that a segment of the Slovak polity sought easy solutions in communist-style monolithism because they had limited familiarity with anything else. They had problems learning to deal with complexity.

## Political Diversity

Although it might seem odd given the polarisation of politics and society in the independent Slovakia, the country may in some respects be seen as less diverse than the Czech Republic. The post-1968 'normalisation' procedure was less brutal in Slovakia than in the Czech Republic, so that the 1968 caesura within the communist period was less marked in Slovakia. This continuity in development has, for example, had an effect on the development of the post-communist parties. The fact that some dynamic elements remained in the Communist Party of Slovakia after 1968 enabled it to modernise and 'social-democratise' itself in the 1990s to the point where it was considered a suitable government coalition partner in 1994 and 1998. In the Czech Republic, however, the inability of the communists to reform themselves is best reflected in their party's name: the Communist Party of Bohemia and Moravia. As a consequence of this failure to reform, former communists have been politically marginalised in the Czech Republic to a very much greater extent than in Slovakia. Slovakia has also shown very much less commitment to the 'lustration' procedure, whereby communists who were active in the former regime are excluded from public office. The suggestion, therefore, is that the Czechs made a far cleaner break with the communist past than the Slovaks. The communist period had also been a more conspicuously negative experience for the Czechs because their pre-communist development had been more positive.

**Ethnic Diversity**

When it comes to ethnic diversity, Slovakia is undoubtedly more divided than the Czech Republic. The 1991 census is somewhat misleading in that it shows the Czech Republic to have a larger ethnic minority (13.2 per cent Moravians) than the Slovak Republic (10.8 per cent Hungarians).[31] A more accurate indicator is mother tongue, which shows 95.8 per cent of citizens in the Czech Republic being Czech speaking (with the remainder largely Slovak speaking), while in the Slovak Republic only 84.3 per cent give Slovak as their mother tongue and 11.5 per cent speak Hungarian.[32] The presence of an ethnic minority has had a more profound effect on the Slovak political agenda because the Hungarians were former imperial rulers, leading to a residual tendency among part of the Slovak elites to define their identity in contradistinction to everything Hungarian. This combines with the fact that the demise of Czechoslovakia was a more divisive issue in Slovakia than in the Czech Republic, and presents politicians with the possibility of pursuing a nationalist agenda. The state is presented as under threat because some of its citizens – the 'Czechoslovakists' and the Hungarians – are not loyal.

**Who are the Elites?**

Problems emerge when one attempts to prove that the factors outlined above have led to the Slovak elites being structurally different from the Czech elites. The most comprehensive elite survey so far conducted in both countries, from the Social Stratification in Eastern Europe project, provides only ambivalent evidence to support this theory.[33] This survey divided the elite into political, economic and culture elites, and compared various characteristics of these elites in 1988 and in 1997. What is most notable in this survey is the differences between the new political elites in the Czech and Slovak Republics. Whereas over 40 per cent of the Slovak political elite were Communist Party members in 1988, and nearly 16 per cent held Communist Party office, for the Czech Republic the figures are only 23 per cent and 1 per cent, respectively. Similarly, compared with the Slovaks, nearly twice as many members of the new Czech political elite sampled (32 per cent) claim to be able to speak English. Interestingly, among the economic and cultural elites, there appear to be more Slovaks than Czechs who could speak English.

It appears, therefore, to be the political agenda that has most differentiated the Czech and Slovak elites in the post-communist period. Two factors are of particular import here, and may explain the rather aberrant Slovak development in the mid-1990s. First, a nationalist agenda was available to Slovak elites because of their relationship to the Czech elites. Slovak development was, in effect, distorted by Czech rule. In particular, Czech privatisation strategies, which denied Slovak economic reality, forced most Slovak politicians to adopt different strategies from their Czech counterparts.[34] The huge resonance of this issue with the public opened up possibilities which could be – and were – exploited by politicians. Once the independent state was founded on the basis of defending national interest, the pressures and insecurities of new statehood together with the presence of a vocal ethnic minority gave a nationally-orientated agenda sufficient momentum to continue. Secondly, the more 'cocooned' and provincial elite operating from Bratislava or other Slovak cities had more affinity with many voters than the more cosmopolitan part of the Slovak elite. The geographic space in which Slovak politics operated provided more scope for political divisions.

## ELITES AND EUROPEAN INTEGRATION

Finally, international factors have constrained the development of elite–public relations in both countries. These have been most politicised in Slovakia, where the failures of the third Mečiar government in achieving its stated aims of European integration were anxiously anticipated by the opposition even before the débâcle of 1997.[35] It was conspicuous that the three parties of Mečiar's governing coalition lacked partners in the West, and were not members of major international organisations. At one point, Slovak political scientists categorised the Slovak political scene as having 'standard' parties (those of the opposition) and 'non-standard' parties (those of the Mečiar government), and membership or non-membership of international organisations was one factor held to distinguish the two categories.[36] The unfortunate response of the Slovak National Party to this typology was to prove that it did have international contacts by forging links to the French Republicans, and inviting their leader to Bratislava.[37]

On the Czech side, the international affiliation of political parties was much clearer. Miloš Zeman's Social Democrats were a natural favourite of the Socialist International, as they were the first social democratic party without roots in a Soviet-era communist party to gain power in the post-communist world. The Klaus governments of 1992–96 and 1996–97 were also both formed of three parties who all belonged to the centre–right European Democratic Union – the Civic Democratic Party, the Christian Democratic Union and the Civic Democratic Alliance. The coherence of the Czech party scene in this regard contrasted markedly with the complexion of the Slovak government from 1998 onwards. The Dzurinda government not only comprised four parliamentary parties ranging from left to right, but one of its components – the Slovak Democratic Coalition – had been formed from parties which belonged to a wide range of different international party organisations.

This was, however, in essence a symptom rather than the cause of Slovakia's initial exclusion from the European integration process. The fundamental problem was that the EU and the conditionality it attached to membership simply allowed no scope for a special 'Slovak path' of transition and modernisation. The European Commission did its utmost to establish objective criteria for the accession of post-communist states but political criteria were paramount, and had to be satisfied before negotiations began, while other criteria had to be met before negotiations ended.[38] Slovakia failed to fulfil the political criteria largely because Mečiar's government was too hostile to pluralism.

The difficulty Slovakia faces is that the EU's demand that there should be 'stability of institutions' is tantamount to requiring an assurance that there will be no political shocks in the future. The little-articulated rule is that there must not be a substantial risk that an election will produce a government unacceptable to the EU. Since alternation of governments is a feature of consolidated democracy, this means that each state must have both a government and an opposition able to act as a competent international partner.

The crucial question then arises of whether the more nationally-minded elites in Slovakia are likely to diminish in size so that the remaining political forces may divide into a left and a right, or whether Mečiar's HZDS and its supporters may metamorphose into a movement which feels more genuine commitment to a European future. It cannot be assumed that the political and economic elites have identical interests in this regard, and the forces which provide financial backing to the HZDS will be prone to distance themselves if the economic disadvantages of the party's policies ever outweigh the political advantages for supporters among the economic elite.

## CONCLUSION

The Czech Republic and Slovakia diverge most markedly at the level of elite behaviour. Whereas Czech elites appear to share a broad consensus about westward integration into international political, military and economic structures, Slovak elites are far more divided, and preoccupied to a higher degree with domestic political contestation.

It can be argued that elite views are more important than popular opinion in determining the functioning of a democracy because elites can manipulate the foci of public opinion. It is therefore the ambivalence and inward-looking agenda of part of the Slovak elite that has played a greater role in delaying the consolidation of Slovak democracy rather than general deficiencies in Slovak political culture. Part of the Slovak elite learnt to mobilise Slovak discontent by concentrating on articulating problems rather than seeking their solutions. How quickly democracy in Slovakia consolidates will depend largely upon the establishment of greater integration between elites, whereby all see each other as legitimate negotiating partners.

However, future developments in both the Czech and Slovak Republics will also depend on the stabilisation of elites. Fluidity of elites and transfer between elites is a feature of post-communism, where few people have extensive training and experience for operating in the conditions of a free market and a democracy.[39] As political, economic and cultural elites become more professionalised and more separate, there is a decreasing likelihood that destructive polarisation of the sort witnessed in Slovakia in the 1990s will continue.

## NOTES

1. See Jiří Musil, 'Czech and Slovak Society', *Government and Opposition*, 28, 4 (1993) pp. 479–95; also in Jiří Musil (ed.), *The End of Czechoslovakia* (Budapest, London, New York 1995) pp. 77–94.
2. See Milada Anna Vachudová and Tim Snyder, 'Are Transitions Transitory? Two Types of Political Change in Eastern Europe Since 1989', *East European Politics and Societies*, 11, 1 (1997) pp. 1–35; Michael Carpenter, 'Slovakia and the Triumph of Nationalist Populism', *Communist and Post-Communist Studies*, 30, 2 (1997) pp. 205–19.
3. See Herbert Kitschelt, 'Formation of Party Cleavages in Post-communist Democracies', *Party Politics*, 1, 4 (1995) pp. 447–72.

4. The European Commission's opinions on the Czech Republic and Slovakia can be found in *Bulletin of the European Union*, Supplements 9/97 and 14/97 (1997).
5. In both Slovakia and the Czech Republic, a 60 per cent majority of all deputies is required in order to change the constitution.
6. See Stephen Whitefield and Geoffrey Evans, 'Political Culture Versus Rational Choice: Explaining Responses to Transition in the Czech Republic and Slovakia', *British Journal of Political Science*, 29, 1 (1999) pp. 129–54; Geoffrey Evans and Stephen Whitefield, 'The Structuring of Political Cleavages in Post-communist Societies: The Case of the Czech Republic and Slovakia', *Political Studies*, 46, 1 (1998) pp. 115–39.
7. See, for example, the 'New Democracies Barometers', most recently Richard Rose and Christian Haerpfer, 'New Democracies Barometer V: A 12-Nation Survey', *Studies in Public Policy*, 306, University of Strathclyde (Glasgow 1998).
8. See, for example, Petr Kopecký and Cas Mudde, 'Growing Apart: Explaining the Different Paths of Democratization in the Czech and Slovak Republics', Paper presented at the 94th Annual American Political Science Convention (Boston, 3–6 September 1998).
9. Karen Henderson, 'Czechoslovakia: The Failure of Consensus Politics and the Break-up of the Federation', *Regional and Federal Studies*, 5, 2 (1995) pp. 111–33.
10. See, for example, Geoffrey Evans and Stephen Whitefield, 'Identifying the Bases of Party Competition in Eastern Europe', *British Journal of Political Science*, 23, 4 (1993) pp. 521–48, which classifies Slovakia as a country with a low chance of market success. No explanation is given for the classification, since it reflects the received wisdom of the time.
11. See Claus Offe, 'Capitalism by Democratic Design? Democratic Theory Facing the Triple Transition in East Central Europe', *Social Research*, 58, 4 (1991) pp. 876–92.
12. Jon Elster, Claus Offe and Ulrich K. Preuss, *Institutional Design in Post-communist Societies: Rebuilding the Ship at Sea* (Cambridge 1998), p.18; see also Attila Ágh, *The Politics of Central Europe* (London 1998) pp. 49—50 and Offe, 'Capitalism by Democratic Design', p.871.
13. Ibid., pp. 869–70.
14. Evans and Whitefield, 'The Structuring of Political Cleavages', p. 121, 126; Herbert Kitschelt, 'Party Systems in East Central Europe: Consolidation or Fluidity', Studies in Public Policy, 241, *University of Strathclyde* (Glasgow 1995) pp. 82–6; Radoslaw Markowski, 'Political Competition and Ideological Dimensions in Central Eastern Europe', *Studies in Public Policy*, 257, University of Strathclyde (Glasgow 1995) p.36; Radoslaw Markowski, 'Political Parties and Ideological Spaces in East Central Europe', *Communist and Post-Communist Studies*, 30, 3 (1997) p. 238.
15. Karen Henderson, 'Divisive Political Agendas: the Case of Czechoslovakia', in Patrick Dunleavy and Jeffrey Stanyer (eds), *Contemporary Political Studies 1994: Proceedings of the Political Studies Association's 1994 Annual Conference* (Belfast 1994) pp. 407–19.
16. Surveys on this subject have been conducted at intervals since 1948. See Archie Brown and Gordon Wightman, 'Czechoslovakia: Revival and Retreat', in Archie

Brown and Jack Gray, *Political Culture and Political Change in Communist States* (London 1997) pp. 159–96; Pavol Frič, Zora Bútorová and Tatiana Rosová, 'Česko-slovenské vzťahy v zrkadle empirického výskumu', *Sociológia*, 24, 1–2 (1992) pp. 43–74; Zora Bútorová and Martin Bútora, 'Events and Personalities in Slovakia's History', in Zora Bútorová (ed.), *Democracy and Discontent in Slovakia: A Public Opinion Profile of a Country in Transition*, Institute for Public Affairs (Bratislava 1998) pp. 191–202.

17. *Bulletin of the European Union*, Supplement 14/97 (1997) p. 20.
18. For details of the spoiled referendum on direct election of the president, see Grigorij Mesežnikov and Martin Bútora (eds.), *Slovenské referendum '97: zrod priebeh, dôsledky*, Inštitút pre verejné otázky (Bratislava 1997).
19. See Karen Henderson and Neil Robinson, *Post-communist Politics* (London 1997) pp. 179–80.
20. Elster et al., *Institutional Design in Post-communist Societies*, pp. 249–51.
21. For a detailed analysis of the 1998 Slovak elections, see Martin Bútora, Grigorij Mesežnikov and Zora Bútorová (eds), *Kto? Prečo? Ako? Slovenské voľby '98*, Inštitút pre verejné otázky (Bratislava 1999).
22. See Ján Bunčák, 'Predstavy o vývoji spoločnosti a spôsoboch jej modernizácie' in Milan Tuček, Ján Bunčák and Valentina Harmadyová (eds), *Statégie a aktéri sociálnej transformácie a modernizácie v Českej a Slovenskej republike*, Doplněk (Brno 1998) pp. 43–67.
23. On the 1998 Czech election, see Karen Henderson, 'Social Democracy Comes to Power: The 1998 Czech Elections', *Labour Focus on Eastern Europe*, 60 (1998) pp. 5–25.
24. See Pavel Machonin, Pavlína Šťastnová, Aleš Kroupa and Alice Glasová, *Strategie sociální transformace české společnosti* (Brno 1996).
25. Czechs in general were also more inclined than Slovaks to regard their Czechoslovak identity to be more important than their Czech identity. See Association for Independent Social Analysis, 'Czechs and Slovaks Compared: A Survey of Economic and Political Behaviour', *Studies in Public Policy*, 198, University of Strathclyde (Glasgow 1992) p. 30.
26. The two leaders concerned are Rudolf Schuster, chair of the Party of Civic Understanding and mayor of Košice, and Ján Slota, chair of the Slovak National Party and mayor of Žilina – both, like Vladimír Mečiar, candidates in the 1999 presidential elections. The fact that mayors are directly elected in Slovakia also has an influence on this development, however.
27. Calculated from Federální statistický úřad, Český statistický úřad, Slovenský štatistický úrad, *Statistick ročenka '91 České a Slovenské federativný republiky* (Prague 1991) p. 695.
28. Although both cities are at opposite ends of their respective countries, the distance between Prague and Brno is approximately 200 km, but between Bratislava and Košice it is 400 km. The long, thin shape of Slovakia, combined with more mountainous terrain, is not naturally conducive to good communications.
29. FOCUS, *Aktuálne problémy Slovenska December 1994* (Bratislava 1994) p. 25.
30. For example, 1997 figures showed that 44 per cent of SDK supporters but only 16 per cent of HZDS supporters could speak at least one Western language. See Bútorová and Bútora, 'Slovakia and the World', in: Bútorová (ed.), *Democracy*

*and Discontent in Slovakia*, pp. 175–89. This can be explained in part by the fact that SDK voters in 1998 were generally younger and better educated. See Oľga Gyárfášová and Miroslav Kúska, 'Vývoj volebných preferencíi a analýza volebného správania', in Bútora, et al., *Kto? Prečo? Ako?*, op. cit., pp. 261–75.

31. Český statistický úřad, *Statistická ročenka České republiky '93* (Prague 1993) p. 412.
32. Ibid., p. 413.
33. For details, see Akos Rona-Tas, Ján Bunčak and Valentina Harmadyova, 'Post-communist Transformation and the New Elite in Slovakia', *Slovak Sociological Review*, 4, 1 (1999).
34. Bunčák, 'Predstavy o vývoji spoločnosti a spôsoboch jej modernizácie', pp. 45–6.
35. The programme of the third Mečiar government published in January 1995 dealt with foreign relations as its first point, and stated the aim of becoming a full member of the EU by the year 2000 as well as joining the 'North Atlantic Alliance' and the European Union. See *Národná obroda* (12 January 1995) p. 9.
36. See Grigorij Mesežnikov, 'The Parliamentary Elections 1994: A Confirmation of the Split of the Party System in Slovakia', in Soňa Szomolányi and Grigorij Mesežnikov (eds), *Slovakia Parliamentary Elections 1994* (Bratislava 1995) pp. 105–6; Grigorij Mesežnikov, 'The Open Ended Formation of Slovakia's Political Party System', in Soňa Szomolányi and John A. Gould (eds.), *Slovakia: Problems of Democratic Consolidation* (Bratislava 1997) p. 43—4.
37. Jean-Marie Le Pen visited Bratislava at the invitation of the chair of SNS in September 1997. HZDS made its disapproval of the visit clear.
38. See Karen Henderson, "Slovakia and the Democratic Criteria for EU Accession", in Karen Henderson (ed.), *Back to Europe: Central and Eastern Europe and the European Union* (London 1999) pp. 221–40.
39. For further discussion of this point, see Elster et al., *Institutional Design in Post-Communst Societies*, pp. 28–34.

# 7. 1 + 1 = 1? The Post-unification East German Elite: Analytical Caveats

## Hans-J. Giessmann

### INTRODUCTION

There can be no doubt that most East Germans appreciated the first chance – when it was given to them – to get rid of the socialist autocracy. Yet the same did not hold for all parts of the upper strata. Indeed, those who had ruled the political system, or profited from the existing political structure, were rather afraid of losing privileges they had enjoyed under socialist rule. But even among these elites, awareness about the achieved deadlock had spread. In particular after Mikhail Gorbachev had come to power in Moscow in 1985, within the intellectual class and even among party officials opinions that only a reform like perestroika could prevent a systemic crash became widespread. However, while growing uneasiness within the public was evident, the party apparatus was still sticking together, critics remained cautious or calm. When the deadlock set in, the elites of the German Democratic Republic (GDR) might have hoped, at least partially, that a political survival through a controlled shift of power – according to a Gorbachev model of perestroika for the GDR – would be possible. As a matter of fact, during the initial phase of transformation, particularly when the first rallies in autumn 1989 took place, prominent intellectuals played an important role in organising campaigns aimed at pressing party and state leaders to initiate reforms.

The situation became different in January 1990 – when the state security police (Stasi) headquarters was stormed – and the public mood shifted away from the idea of transforming socialism within the boundaries of the GDR towards the idea of a rapid unification, which was given expression by the motto of mass rallies 'We are *the* people' becoming 'We are *one* people'. The overwhelming public vote for unity resulted in a clear victory for the conservative 'Alliance for Germany' in the March 1990 elections. The victory of the Christian Alliance immediately transferred the political initiative of transformation from (East) Berlin to Bonn. Thereafter the leading role of intellectual eastern reformers became marginalised. Political representatives were absorbed by the West German party establishment. During the phase of public euphoria this change within the East German political landscape did not matter greatly, at least as long as most people considered a rapid unification to be the best choice for achieving more democracy and improved living conditions in the short run. This changed, however, when the same people experienced unification for the first time rather as a shock than a blessing. All of a sudden many people felt dominated against their will by political decisions taken in Bonn and they began to miss appropriate representation of their interests and concerns within the process of federal decision making.

The combination of transformation and unification posed a particular dilemma for the East German elites. The old political elite was compromised; it was removed from power and its previous influence. The former intellectual elite was more or less paralysed by the perceived defeat of their aspirations and ideas of political change with the prospect of still having a GDR state. On the other hand, the group of fresh reformers was small, inexperienced, heterogeneous and eventually too weak to become acknowledged by the western party establishment as being really equal. While those reformers who joined the western establishment faced political and structural problems of exerting eastern influence on federal policy, the caucus of a new East German elite became more and more influenced by criticism of what was perceived to be western domination.

Ironically, approximately a decade after unification, and notwithstanding substantial successes in economic and social transformation, the further existence of rifts within German society between east and west cannot be ignored, some of which have even arisen or become deeper only since 1990. What may be called the East German elite as of today is reflecting these rifts, because it is neither existing nor acting in a political vacuum. It may be interesting to analyse whether the newly emerging signs of a corporate identity among the East German elite can be seen as a transitional reflection of a process of 'inner unification' or as a fairly stable reflection of a different political, social, economic and cultural environment in both east and west. If the first is true it may be worthwhile to elaborate on the nature and pace of transformation in East Germany in comparison with the adopted western standards. If the latter is true it would be necessary to identify the reasons for such differences and perhaps also to draw conclusions regarding their impact on the nation-building process in Germany as a whole. In this chapter, however, I shall argue that the East German transformation phenomenon lends some truth to both assumptions.

## THE COMPOSITION OF THE EAST GERMAN ELITE

Analysis of the East German elite and of its responses to transformation must be prefaced by several caveats. The notion of 'elite' embraces individuals and institutions which exert substantial influence on political decision making, economic performance and development, and also on the cultural cohesion of a society. Therefore policy makers, top managers, university professors, novelists, military commanders and others comprise the heterogeneous group of a nation's elite.

A first caveat regarding the East German elite, however, is related to its composition. One may even question whether there is a genuine East German elite at all. The previous 'political elite' has practically disappeared. Most of them were removed from top-ranking posts in political and state administration. Either they were retired or replaced by a new generation of younger reformers or by so-called 'imports' from the west. Yet several members of the former bureaucratic elites have managed to take over executive positions in the field of small or medium business, by making use of specific competitive advantages, such as better information or their privileged access to capital and loans during the initial phase of transition. Such 'transfers' scarcely took place in other realms. The military and security structures were refashioned almost from scratch. Yet some 'transfers' from the military and security apparatus into the free market economy have been reported as well. But in contrast to the political realm in the military there was no similar replacement of top-ranking positions by eastern reformers. Party membership and loyalty were essential prerequisites for any appointment to high-ranking positions in the GDR military. Any signs of criticism usually ended in people being dismissed without notice. That is why all staff and field commanders, all generals and also most colonels of the former National People's Army and Police were fired and replaced by 'imports' from the west. The state security police (Stasi) was completely dissolved.

Replacement in the area of research and university teaching – particularly but not only in social sciences – was similarly radical. Approximately 80 per cent of all tenured positions at East German universities were given to professors of West German origin. In political science the rate of replacement amounted to almost 100 per cent.

At first glance the least changes affected leading personalities in culture and the arts. Their cutomary freelance status provided protection against political compromise, except for those who were members of the politico-cultural administration. Yet the free influx of 'western culture' after unification and the new situation of harder competition for economic survival contributed to a marginalisation of the previously privileged eastern 'cultural class'. Apart from that, sharply shrinking state and local subsidies for culture and also the distress of previous consumers made it increasingly difficult for those involved in arts to accumulate the funds necessary for the survival of theatres, bookshops, opera houses and so on. Moreover, many of them had great difficulties in adjusting themselves to the new environment after the 'cultural biotop' of the GDR had evaporated.

Preliminary conclusions can be drawn as follows. The reconstitution of the East German elite after unification was characterised by intrusive but asymmetric changes, whose typical features are elimination, transfer, import and adjustment. This makes it very difficult to compare elite attitudes today with those of the late GDR.

## ELITES AND SOCIAL STRATA

A second caveat might be called an ambivalent link between the elites and the social strata. Elites do not act in a political vacuum. Their power and influence are dependent on an enduring ability to reflect and to respond to public attitudes, and to maintain public support. If elites become estranged they run the risk of losing their own constituency. As for East Germany after unification, the change (replacements) within the elites was very strongly influenced by the dominating part which the old Federal Republic was bound to play in the transition process. In contrast to other reforming countries in Central Europe, there was very little room for creating a kind of self-renewal within the East German elites.

Apart from the problems mentioned above, the structural replacement at the top occurred in a radical and immediate way, not least as a result of the pressures from unification simultaneous. While the transition of power led more or less simply to a radical substitution of individuals and institutions, most ordinary people had to rebuild their careers from scratch by adjusting to a rapidly changing environment. Many people experienced the transformation of their lives in a non-democratic way – imposed by decision making from above – which resulted in a gradual alienation between the top and the grassroots, the masses and the elites, and, at least temporarily, resulted in shaken confidence on the part of many people in the credibility of justice and democracy. Growing tensions between perceived federal ('western') standards and regional ('eastern') reality were increasingly reflected among the new elites, especially in the realm of state and local politics. For those who were in charge at local level the striking gap of perception between the promise of 'blooming landscapes' (Helmut Kohl) and the troublesome reality become a political challenge to their own credibility and legitimacy. This challenge also became physically existent: the post-communist Party of Democratic Socialism (PDS) did not disappear but managed to mobilise both old and new constituencies. The democratic parties did not realise at this point that voting for the PDS was by no means motivated only by nostalgic feelings but also by uneasiness about how the process of unification was managed. While the PDS was bluntly blamed simply for having its communist past – and therefore no legitimacy at all in a pluralist democracy – an open discussion about the substance and the contradictions was therefore missed. Moreover, the diverse reasons for voting for the PDS were not considered. Under such circumstances it was easy for the PDS to attract a strong constituency with populist and anti-western slogans.

But the process of political differentiation is not only due to the existence of the PDS. The gap between original expectations and wishes on the one hand, and the difficulties of transformation on the other has affected all democratic elites. The many politicians, managers, journalists and editors who have moved from west to east during the 1990s have become more and more susceptible to the idea of a corporate 'eastern' identity, even risking harsh disputes with their own western compatriots. Many of these 'westerners' – who have experienced East German reality at first hand – have been 'transformed' into 'easterners'. Of course, such a distinction is never clear-cut, and the issue of a corporate identity should not be overestimated. However, if eastern politicians argue that the transfer of the Federal government from Bonn to Berlin might help West Germans better understand the structural difficulties of inner unification, it becomes clear that traditional east-contra-west images still matter.

## ONE NATION – TWO POLITICAL CULTURES?

A third caveat is connected with the political culture in East Germany. The peaceful transition of power created, *inter alia*, the culture of the 'round-table' – which for many East Germans was the first experience of the modalities of democracy. With rapid unification the shoots of grassroots democracy and self-determination were stifled by the well-functioning and well-established West German party system. Most of the democratic proto-parties of the months of change either ceased to exist or became absorbed by the established parties. The rate of active political participation of East Germans dropped sharply. For example, while one person out of ten in West Germany is a member of the Social Democratic Party (SPD), only one person out of 200,000 in East Germany is amember. Similar discrepancies can be detected with regard to the Christian Democrats, the Free Democrats and the Greens. The only party with a large membership in East Germany is the PDS, with approximately one party member per 16 inhabitants. Yet the common perception in the west, that the strong support for the post-communists primarily reflects nostalgic feelings and memories is erroneous. Most surveys show that only a negligible proportion of East Germans (1–2 per cent) favour a return to the GDR reality.

A complex transformation of a society cannot be seen simply as a clear-cut road from A to B. There is good reason to assume that many voters of the PDS do not fully support the party's populist and anti-western programme, but do not see another party offering a plausible alternative, particularly if their difficult individual living conditions are considered. It would also be inaccurate to regard the fairly stable support for the PDS by almost one-quarter of the population in the new *Länder* as simply a vote by 'losers'. It is the poor performance of the established parties rather than a good performance of the PDS, and a spreading dissatisfaction with the slow pace of economic and social improvement, which accounts for the different voting in East Germany. This dissatisfaction also explains why a comparatively large number of East Germans vote for extreme right parties, although they are no more radical than their western fellow-countrymen.

Ten years after unification it has become clear that transformation in the new *Länder* will take much longer than the transfer of power. While the latter has already been achieved, transformation is still in a state of flux – as are the responses of the incoherent and regrouping elites in East Germany to the changing reality. Spot checks cannot provide plausible and sufficient explanations for the process of change. Only long-term observation may help us to understand better the causes of existing rifts within the society and to assess the chances of eventually achieving what is called 'inner unification'.

## PHASES OF TRANSFORMATION

Political sociologists have detected three phases of transformation in East Germany so far, each accompanied by different public attitudes and elite responses.[1] The first phase began in early 1990 and lasted barely a year. It was characterised by widespread euphoria about unification and by far-reaching expectations and hopes for liberalism, economic prosperity and social welfare. It ended with the 'unification shock', which marked the beginning of a second phase of transformation. This shock was triggered by a rude awakening, especially when the real East German economic situation became apparent, and when (western) federal law was applied to the new *Länder* after October 1990. Apart from sharply rising (and never before experienced) unemployment it was primarily the issue of the restitution of land (2.5 million applications within two years) which led to sobering attitudes about unification in East Germany. It can be argued *ex post facto* that the issue of restitution probably produced the core of what has later been seen as deeply rooted anti-western resentment within large sections of the East German society. To understand structural differences between East Germany and other reforming societies in Central Europe it is important to consider the huge significance of the property issue for those millions of East Germans who now saw the society of which they had wished to become a part as a threat to their previous achievements. The third – and still continuing – phase of transformation started in about the year 1994, and can be described as 'post-shock accommodation'.

Public surveys in East Germany have shown a direct link between the general acceptance of democracy and the perception of transformation and its results. While the general acceptance of democracy within East Germany has always been very high, the 'West German' type of democracy has not attracted the same support. The reason for this discrepancy is twofold.

First of all, unification has been experienced by many people as a one-way street. The accession of the five *Länder* to the Federal Republic, according to Article 23 of their Basic Law, led to the application of this West German law in East Germany – with a few transitional exceptions according to the unity treaty which was concluded by the Federal government and the government of the GDR. While during the period of the 'round table' talks East Germans 'learned' democracy from scratch, the results of these talks quickly vanished into thin air when the legal framework of the Federal Republic was applied to East Germany. Many people felt deprived of the democratic achievements they had accomplished during the short period of democratisation in the late GDR.

Second, and more importantly, many were confronted with what they perceived to be a second-class citizen image, following a devaluation of their status, education and individual achievements within the autocratic socialist past. Some party leaders such as the chairmen of both the Christian Democratic Union (CDU)–East and the SPD–East · faced allegations of former collaboration with the Stasi. This not only contributed a great deal to a narrowing of the public debate about unification to the question of Stasi files but also reduced the legitimacy of the eastern democratic movement within the process of unification as a whole. While only about 100,000 persons may have collaborated with the secret police, millions of innocent people were suspected of having had contacts with the Stasi. Moreover, apart from the property issue, the nascent economic restructuring was also experienced as one-sided. Several scandals which accompanied the activities of the *Treuhand* – in connection with the closing down of East German industries – contributed to a general impression that the west was more interested in short-term gain than in long-run economic rehabilitation.

While the overall acceptance of democracy as the best political system has remained stable above 80 per cent, acceptance of the German democratic reality after unification peaked in 1990 with a rate of 58 per cent, but dropped during the unification shock period to only 33 per cent. Since 1994 acceptance has begun to recover, though it has not yet achieved the peak level of 1990 again.[2] It has been a widely shared assumption by politicians and social scientists that with an improving standard of living in the east negative perceptions of democratic reality would disappear. If this assumption holds true, it will surely take a long time to come about. More than 60 per cent of East Germans believe that their living conditions are worse, when compared with their own GDR past. When asked whether they feel like second-class Germans, 87 per cent have answered 'yes' in 1990, decreasing to 67 per cent in 1995, but increasing again to 80 per cent in 1997.[3]

Having said that, the standard of living alone cannot serve as a sufficient indicator for the existing societal rifts in East Germany and between east and west. One may even argue that similar striking differences in terms of income and welfare on average exist between northern and southern states of West Germany. While there can be no doubt that in social terms – and also in economic terms – the situation in East Germany has become significantly better, other factors still matter, perhaps even more now than before, which contradict the hypothesis mentioned above. Moreover, the process of transformation is not linear in nature, but shows signs of unstable waves. These may point to structural asymmetries in the transformation of values within the society. Results of sociological analyses in 1996 have revealed that at least three out of four East Germans are totally or partly disappointed with the progress of inner unification.[4]

Jobs and the high rate of crime and violence are top priorities on the agenda of concerns of most East Germans. Other traditional fields of domestic political competition – such as equal rights for women, ecology and middle-class issues – matter much less in the east than in the west. Neither the federal Democratic Party nor the Greens enjoy strong support in the new *Länder*. Compared with the early 1990s both parties have lost seats in most state and local parliaments. The political structure in the new *Länder* has become more or less tripolar – Christian Democrats, Social Democrats and post-communists – and there is no sign that this situation will will change in the near future.

The delicate political balance within this tripolar situation reduces the options for democratic choice. It became obvious after the elections of 1998 that either grand coalitions of Christian and Social Democrats or Red–Red coalitions of Social Democrats and the PDS represented the only alternatives, at least at national level. Ironically, at local levels fears of involvement matter much less. There we find many forms of pragmatic coalitions, even between the CDU and the PDS, which can largely be explained by the positive experiences people had during the 'round table' talks. It can be concluded that the grassroots political culture has survived to a large extent at local levels. Therefore, the composition of local elites is not mirroring the traditional democratic culture of the Federal Republic.

In general it can be concluded that the process of the transition of power has been smooth and without substantial problems. Democracy in East Germany has successfully stood the test of social transformation and can be evaluated as stable. However, democracy at local levels is still showing signs of the transitory culture of 'round tables'. Impediments to coalitions among political opponents are apparently weaker in the east, not least in order to generate broad legitimacy for pushing ahead pragmatic projects of common interest against what is seen to be 'negative influence from above' on local or regional issues. In that respect the PDS will probably play a long-term role in the elite-building process in East Germany. One may argue that this implies enduring tension between east and west. However, one may also argue that similar rifts can be found in West Germany, for example between Bavaria and NorthRhine-Westphalia, and that such features will finally contribute rather to an enrichment of German democracy.

## NOTES

1. See Rolf Reissig, ,'Was wollen die Ostdeutschen', mimeo (Hamburg April 1997) pp. 1–18.
2. See ApuZ, B 51/97, p. 5 (Allensbach 1997).
3. Ibid., p. 13.
4. See Reissig, ,'Was wollen die Ostdeutchen'.

# Bibliography

Agh, Attila, *The Politics of Central Europe* (London: Sage, 1998).

Aghion, Philippe and Oliver Jean Blanchard, 'On the Speed of Transition in Central Europe', EBRD Working Paper, 6, European Bank for Reconstruction and Development (London 1993).

ApuZ, B 51/97 (Allensbach 1997).

Åslund, Anders, Peter Boone and Simon Johnson, 'How to Stabilize: Lessons from Post-Communist Countries', *Brookings Papers on Economic Activity*, 1 (1996).

Association for Independent Social Analysis, 'Czechs and Slovaks Compared: A Survey of Economic and Political Behaviour', Studies in Public Policy, 198, *University of Strathclyde* (Glasgow 1992).

Aziz, Jahangir and Robert F. Wescott, 'Policy Complementarities and the Washington Consensus', IMF Working Paper, 97/118, International Monetary Fund (Washington DC 1997).

Balcerowicz, Leszek, *Socialism, Capitalism, Transformation* (Budapest: Central European University Press, 1995).

Bardhan, Pranab, 'The Nature of Institutional Impediments to Economic Development', mimeo, University of California at Berkeley (Berkeley CA 1995).

Barro, Robert J., *Determinants of Economic Growth: A Cross-country Empirical Study* (Cambridge MA 1997).

Barro, Robert J. and Xavier Sala-i-Martin, *Economic Growth* (New York: McGraw-Hill, 1995).

Barry, Brian and Russil Hardin (eds), *Rational Man and Irrational Society: An Introduction and Source Book* (Beverly Hills: Sage, 1982).

Bartlett, David L., *The Political Economy of Dual Transformations: Market Reform and Democratization in Hungary* (Ann Arbor MI: University of Michigan Press, 1997).

Berg, Andrew, Eduardo Borensztein, Ratna Sahay and Jeromin Zettelmeyer, 'The Evolution of Output in Transition Economies – Explaining the Differences', IMF Working Paper, 99/73, International Monetary Fund (Washington DC 1999).

Bird, Graham, 'The International Monetary Fund and Developing Countries: A Review of the Evidence and Policy Options', *International Organization*, 50, 3 (1996).

Bjork, James, 'The Uses of Conditionality: Poland and the IMF', *East European Quarterly*, 39, 1 (1995).

Blanchard, Oliver, *The Economics of Transition in Eastern Europe* (Oxford: Oxford University Press, 1997).

Bönker, Frank, 'The Political Economy of Fiscal Reform in Eastern Europe', mimeo, Humboldt University (Berlin 1999).

Bosworth, Barry, 'The Asian Financial Crisis', *The Brookings Review*, 16, 3 (1998).

Boycko, Maxim, Andrei Shleifer and Robert W.. Vishny, 'Second-best Economic Policy for a Divided Government', *European Economic Review*, 40 (1996).

Boycko, Maxim, Andrei Shleifer, and Robert W. Vishny, *Privatizing Russia* (Cambridge MA: MIT Press, 1995).

Bratton, Michael and Nicholas van de Walle, 'Toward Governance in Africa: Popular Demands and State Responses', in Goran Hydén and Michael Bratton (eds), *Governance and Politics in Africa* (Boulder CO: Westview Press, 1992).

Brown, Archie and Gordon Wightman, 'Czechoslovakia: Revival and Retreat', in Archie Brown and Jack Gray, *Political Culture and Political Change in Communist States* (London: Macmillan, 1997).

Brunetti, Aymo, Gregory Kisunko and Beatrice Weder, 'Credibility of Rules and Economic Growth: Evidence From a Worldwide Survey of the Private Sector', Policy Research Working Paper, 1760, World Bank (Washington DC 1997).

Bruno, Michael, 'Stabilization and Reform in Eastern Europe after Communism', *IMF Staff Paper*, 39 (1992).

Bruno, Michael and William Easterly, 'Inflation Crises and Long-run Growth', *Journal of Monetary Economics*, 41 (1998).

*Bulletin of the European Union*, Supplements 9/97 and 14/97 (1997).

Bunčák, Ján, 'Predstavy o vývoji spoločnosti a spôsoboch jej modernizácie', in Milan Tuček, Ján Bunčák and Valentina Harmadyová, *Statégie a aktéri sociálnej transformácie a modernizácie v Českej a Slovenskej republike*, Doplněk (Brno 1998).

*Business Central Europe*, various issues.

Bútora, Martin, Grigorij Mesežnikov and Zora Bútorová (eds), *Kto? Prečo? Ako? Slovenské voľby '98*, Inštitút pre verejné otázky (Bratislava 1999).

Bútorová, Zora and Martin Bútora, 'Slovakia and the World', in Zora Bútorová (ed.), *Democracy and Discontent in Slovakia: A Public Opinion Profile of a Country in Transition*, Institute for Public Affairs (Bratislava 1998).

Bútorová, Zora and Martin Bútora, 'Events and Personalities in Slovakia's History', in Zora Bútorová (ed.), *Democracy and Discontent in Slovakia: A Public Opinion Profile of a Country in Transition*, Institute for Public Affairs (Bratislava 1998).

Campos, Jose Edgardo and Hilton L. Root, *The Key to the Asian Miracle: Making Shared Growth Credible* (Washington DC: The Brookings Institution, 1996).

Carpenter, Michael, 'Slovakia and the Triumph of Nationalist Populism', *Communist and Post-Communist Studies*, 30, 2 (1997).

Cassard, Marcel and David Folkerts-Landau, 'Sovereign Debt: Managing the Risks', *Finance and Development* (1997).

Český statistický úřad, *Statistická ročenka České republiky '93* (Prague 1993).

Christoffersen, Peter and Peter Doyle, 'From Inflation to Growth: Eight Years of Transition', IMF Working Paper, International Monetary Fund (Washington DC 1999).

'Coordinating Reforms in the Public Sector: Improving Performance and Combating Corruption', Briefing Notes on a Workshop Organised by the Government of Georgia with the Assistance of the World Bank (June 1998).

Corbo, Vittorio and Stanley Fischer, 'Adjustment Programs and Bank Support: Rationale and Main Results', Policy, Research, and External Affairs Working Papers, Country Economics Department of the World Bank (Washington DC 1991).

Coricelli, Fabrizio, *Macroeconomic Policies and Development of Markets in Transition Economies* (Budapest: Central European University Press, 1998).

Cranenburgh, Oda van, 'Increasing State Capacity. What Role for the World Bank?', *IDS Bulletin*, 29, 2 (1998).

Csaba, László, 'Hungary and the IMF: The Experience of Cordial Discord', *Journal of Comparative Economics*, 20, 2 (1995).

*Current Digest of the Post-Soviet Press*, 51, 7 (1999).

Dahl, Robert A., *Who Governs? Democracy and Power in American Cities* (New Haven: Yale University Press, 1961).

De Haan, Jakob and Clemens Siermann, 'Luxury or Stimulus? The Impact of Democracy on Economic Growth', mimeo, University of Groningen (Groningen 1995).

De Melo, Martha, Cevdet Denizer and Alan Gelb, 'From Plan to Market: Patterns of Transition', Policy Research Department, Transition Economics Division, *The World Bank* (Washington DC 1996).

De Melo, Martha, Cevdet Denizer, Alan Gelb and Stoyan Tenev, 'Circumstance and Choice: The Role of Initial Conditions and Policies in Transition Economies', *International Finance Corporation* (Washington DC 1997).

Desai, Padma, 'Macroeconomic Fragility and Exchange Rate Vulnerability: A Cautionary Record of Transition Economies', *Journal of Comparative Economics*, 26, 4 (1998).

Dixit, Avinash, *The Making of Economic Policy: A Transaction-cost Perspective* (Cambridge MA: MIT Press, 1996).

Drábek, Zdenek, 'IMF and IBRD Policies in the Former Czechoslovakia', *Journal of Comparative Economics*, 20, 2 (1995).

*Eastern European Newsletter*, various issues.

*The Economist*, various issues.

Eggertsson, Thráinn, *Economic Behavior and Institutions* (Cambridge: Cambridge University Press, 1990).

Elster, Jon, Claus Offe and Ulrich K. Preuss, *Institutional Design in Post-communist Societies: Rebuilding the Ship at Sea* (Cambridge: Cambridge University Press, 1998)

European Bank for Reconstruction and Development, *The Political Aspects of the Mandate of the EBRD* (London 1992).

European Bank for Reconstruction and Development, *Transition Report* (London, various years).

Evans, Geoffrey Evans and Stephen Whitefield, 'Identifying the Bases of Party Competition in Eastern Europe', *British Journal of Political Science*, 23, 4 (1993).

Evans, Geoffrey and Stephen Whitefield, 'The Structuring of Political Cleavages in Post-Communist Societies: The Case of the Czech Republic and Slovakia', *Political Studies*, 46, 1 (1998).

Federální statistický úřad, Český statistický úřad, Slovenský štatistický úrad, *Statistick ročenka '91 České a Slovenské federativný republiky* (Prague 1991).

*Financial Times*, various issues.

Fischer, Stanley, 'The Role of Macroeconomic Factors in Growth', *Journal of Monetary Economics*, 32 (1993).

Fischer Stanley, 'ABCDE: Tenth Conference Address', speech presented at the World Bank Annual Bank Conference on Development Economics, World Bank (Washington DC April 1998).

Fischer, Stanley and Alan Gelb, 'The Process of Socialist Economic Transformation', *Journal of Economic Perspectives*, 5, 4 (1991).

Fischer, Stanley, Ratna Sahay and Carlos A. Végh, 'Stabilization and Growth in Transition Economies: The Early Experience', *Journal of Economic Perspectives*, 10, 2 (1996).

FOCUS, *Aktuálne problémy Slovenska December 1994* (Bratislava 1994).

*Foreign Policy*, various issues.

Frey, Bruno, S., *Modern Political Economy* (Oxford: Martin Robertson, 1978).

Frič, Pavol, Zora Bútorová and Tatiana Rosová, 'Česko-slovenské vzfahy v zrkadle empirického výskumu', *Sociológia*, 24, 1–2 (1992).

Frischtak, Leila L. 'Governance Capacity and Economic Reform in Developing Countries', World Bank Technical Paper, 254, World Bank (Washington DC 1994).

Frohlich, Norman, Joe A. Oppenheimer and Oran R. Young, *Political Leadership and Collective Goods*, (Princeton 1971).

Ghosh, Atish, and Steven Phillips, 'Inflation, Disinflation, and Growth', IMF Working Paper, 98/68, *International Monetary Fund* (Washington DC 1998).

Gomulka, Stanislaw, 'The IMF-Supported Programs of Poland and Russia, 1990– 1994: Principles, Errors, and Results', *Journal of Comparative Economics*, 20, 3 (1995).

Grindle, Merilee S. and Mary E. Hilderbrand 'Building Sustainable Capacity in the Public Sector: What Can Be Done?', *Public Administration and Development*, 15 (1995).

Gyárfášová Oľga and Miroslav Kúska, 'Vývoj volebných preferencíi a analýza volebného správania', in Martin Bútora, Grigorij Mesežnikov and Zora Bútorová (eds), *Kto? Prečo? Ako? Slovenské voľby '98*, Inštitút pre verejné otázky (Bratislava 1999).

Haggard, Stephan, 'The Politics of Adjustment: Lessons from the IMF's Extended Fund Facility', in Miles Kahler (ed.), *The Politics of International Debt* (Ithaca: Cornell University Press, 1986)

Haggard, Stephan, Marc Levy, Andrew Moravcsik and Kalypso Nicolaidis, 'Integrating the Two Halves of Europe: Theories of Interests, Bargaining, and Institutions', in Robert Keohane, Joseph Nye, and Stanley Hoffmann (eds), *After the Cold War: International Institutions and State Strategies in Europe, 1989— 1991* (Cambridge MA: Harvard University Press, 1993).

Harberger, Arnold C., 'A Vision of the Growth Process', *The American Economic Review*, 88, 1 (1998).

Hare, Paul G., 'The Distance between Eastern Europe and Brussels: Reform Deficits in Potential Member States', in Horst Siebert (ed.), *Quo Vadis Europe?* (Tübingen 1997).

Havrylyshyn, Oleh and Peter Botousharov, 'Five Years of Transition', *Bank Review*, 4, Bulgarian National Bank (Sofia 1995).

Hellman, Joel S., 'Winners Take All. The Politics of Partial Reform in Postcommunist Transitions', *World Politics*, 50 (1998).

Henderson, Karen, 'Divisive Political Agendas: The Case of Czechoslovakia', in Patrick Dunleavy and Jeffrey Stanyer (eds.), *Contemporary Political Studies 1994: Proceedings of the Political Studies Association's 1994 Annual Conference* (Belfast 1994).

Henderson, Karen, 'Czechoslovakia: The Failure of Consensus Politics and the Break-up of the Federation', *Regional and Federal Studies*, 5, 2 (1995).

Henderson, Karen, 'Social Democracy Comes to Power: The 1998 Czech Elections', *Labour Focus on Eastern Europe*, 60 (1998).

Henderson, Karen, 'Slovakia and the Democratic Criteria for EU Accession', in Karen Henderson (ed.), *Back to Europe: Central and Eastern Europe and the European Union* (London: UCL Press, 1999).

Henderson, Karen and Neil Robinson, *Post-Communist Politics* (London: Prentice-Hall, 1997).

Hernández-Catá, Ernesto, 'Liberalization and the Behavior of Output During the Transition from Plan to Market', IMF Working Paper, 97/53, International Monetary Fund (Washington DC 1997).

Hiemenz, Ulrich, 'Development Strategies and Foreign Aid Policies for Low Income Countries in the 1990s', Kiel Discussion Papers, 152, Kiel Institute of World Economics (Kiel 1989).

Hoen, Herman W., *The Transformation of Economic Systems in Central Europe* (Cheltenham, UK: Edward Elgar, 1998).

Honeywell, Martin, *The Poverty Brokers: The IMF and Latin America* (London 1983).

Hydén, Goran, 'Governance and the Study of Politics', in Goran Hydén and Michael Bratton (eds) *Governance and Politics in Africa* (Boulder CO 1992).

*International Herald Tribune*, various issues.

International Monetary Fund, 'Good Governance. The IMF's Role' (Washington DC 1997).

International Monetary Fund, 'Growth Experiences in Transition Economies', SM/98/228 (Washington DC 1998).

James, Harold, 'From Grandmotherliness to Governance. The Evolution of IMF Conditionality', *Finance and Development*, 35, 4 (1998).

Johnson, Simon, Daniel Kaufmann and Andrei Shleifer, 'The Unofficial Economy in Transition', *Brookings Papers on Economic Activity,* 2 (1997).

Kahler, Miles, 'External Influence, Conditionality, and the Politics of Adjustment', in Stephan Haggard and Robert Kaufmann (eds), *The Politics of Economic Adjustment* (Princeton 1992).

Killick, Tony, 'Principals, Agents and the Limitations of BWI Conditionality', *World Economy*, 19 (1996).

Kitschelt, Herbert, 'Formation of Party Cleavages in Post-Communist Democracies', *Party Politics*, 1, 4 (1995).

Kitschelt, Herbert, Party Systems in East Central Europe: Consolidation or Fluidity, *Studies in Public Policy*, 241, University of Strathclyde (Glasgow 1995)

Kjaer, Mette, 'Governance – Making It Tangible', paper presented at the 'Good Governance' working group at the EADI Conference (Vienna 11–14 September 1996).

Knack, Stephen and Philip Keefer, 'Does Social Capital Have an Economic Payoff? A Cross-Country Investigation', *Quarterly Journal of Economics,* 112, 4 (1997).

Kopecký, Petr and Cas Mudde, 'Growing Apart: Explaining the Different Paths of Democratization in the Czech and Slovak Republics', Paper presented at the 94th Annual American Political Science Convention (Boston, 3–6 September 1998).

Kornai, János, 'Transformational Recession: The Main Causes', *Journal of Comparative Economics*, 19 (1994).

Krueger, Anne O., 'The Political Economy of a Rent-Seeking Society', *American Economic Review*, 64, 3 (1974).

Lancaster, Carol, 'Governance and Development: The Views from Washington', IDS *Bulletin*, 24, 1 (1993).

Landell-Mills, Pierre and Ismail Serageldin, 'Governance and the External Factor', *Proceedings of the World Bank Annual Conference on Development Economics 1991* (Washington DC 1992).

Lavigne, Marie, *The Economics of Transition: From Socialist Economy to Market Economy* (Basingstoke: Macmillan, 1999).

Leisinger, Klaus M., 'Gouvernanz oder: 'Zuhause muß beginnen, was leuchten soll im Vaterland', in Klaus M. Leisinger, Vittorio Hösle (eds), *Entwicklung mit menschlichem Antlitz. Die Dritte und die Erste Welt im Dialog* (Munich: Beck, 1995).

Leonard, David K., 'Professionalism and African Administration', *IDS Buulletin*, 24, 1 (1993).

Machonin, Pavel, Pavlína Šťastnová, Aleš Kroupa and Alice Glasová, *Strategie sociální transformace české společnosti* (Brno 1996).

Markowski, Radoslaw, 'Political Competition and Ideological Dimensions in Central Eastern Europe', *Studies in Public Policy*, 257, University of Strathclyde (Glasgow 1995).

Markowski, Radoslaw, 'Political Parties and Ideological Spaces in East Central Europe', *Communist and Post-Communist Studies*, 30, 3 (1997).

Martimort, David, 'The Multiprinciple Nature of Government', *European Economic Review*, 40 (1996).

Martin, Denis-Constant, 'The Cultural Dimensions of Governance', *Proceedings of the World Bank Annual Conference on Development Economics 1991* (Washington DC 1992).

Meltzer, Allan, 'Asian Problems and the IMF', *Cato Journal*, 17, 3 (1998).

Mesežnikov, Grigorije, 'The Parliamentary Elections 1994: A Confirmation of the Split of the Party System in Slovakia', in: Soňa Szomolányi and Grigorij Mesežnikov (eds.), *Slovakia Parliamentary Elections 1994* (Bratislava1995).

Mesežnikov, Grigorij and Martin Bútora (eds), *Slovenské referendum '97: zrod priebeh, dôsledky*, Inštitút pre verejné otázky (Bratislava 1997).

Mesežnikov, Grigorij, 'The Open Ended Formation of Slovakia's Political Party System', in Soňa Szomolányi and John A. Gould (eds), *Slovakia: Problems of Democratic Consolidation* (Bratislava 1997).

Miller-Adams, Michelle, 'The World Bank in the 1990s: Understanding Institutional Change', Paper Presented at the Annual Meeting of the American Political Science Association (San Francisco 1996).

Mills, C. Wright, *The Power Elite* (New York: Oxford University Press, 1956).

Moore, Mick, 'Declining to Learn from the East? The World Bank on "Governance and Development"', IDS B*ulletin*, 24, 1 (1993).

Mosley, Paul, Jane Herrigan and John Toye, *Aid and Power: The World Bank and Policy-based Lending* (London: Routledge, 1991).

Mummert, Uwe, 'Making institutions work: from *de jure* to *de facto* institutional reform', Paper presented at the IAES conference (Vienna, 17–22 March 1999).

Murrell, Peter, 'Evolutionary and Radical Approaches to Economic Reform', *Economics of Planning*, 25 (1992) pp. 79–95.

Murell, Peter and Mancur Olson, 'The Devolution of Centrally Planned Economies', *Journal of Comparative Economics*, 15 (1991).

Musil, Jiří, 'Czech and Slovak Society', *Government and Opposition*, 28.4 (1993).

Musil, Jiří (ed.), *The End of Czechoslovakia* (Budapest, London, New York: Central European University Press, 1995).

*Národná obroda* (12 January 1995).

Nicolaidis, Kalypso, 'East European Trade in the Aftermath of 1989: Did International Institutions Matter?', in Robert Keohane, Joseph Nye and Stanley Hoffmann (eds), *After the Cold War: International Institutions and State Strategies in Europe, 1989–1991* (Cambridge MA: Harvard University Press, 1993).

North, Douglass C. 'Institutions, Ideology, and Economic Performance', *Cato Journal*, 11, 3 (1992).

North, Douglass C., 'Some Fundamental Puzzles in Economic History / Development', unpublished manuscript, Washington University (St. Louis 1995).

Nunberg, Barbara, *The State After Communism. Administrative Transitions in Central and Eastern Europe*, The World Bank (Washington DC 1999).

Nunnenkamp, Peter, 'What Donors Mean by Good Governance: Heroic Ends, Limited Means, and Traditional Dilemmas of Development Cooperation', *IDS Bulletin*, 26, 2 (1995).

Offe, Claus, 'Capitalism by Democratic Design? Democratic Theory Facing the Triple Transition in East Central Europe', *Social Research*, 58, 4 (1991).

Olson, Mancur, *The Logic of Collective Action* (Cambridge MA: Harvard University Press, 1965).

Olson, Mancur, *The Rise and Decline of Nations. Economic Growth, Stagflation and Social Rigidities* (New Haven: Yale University Press, 1982).

Olson, Mancur, 'The Hidden Path to a Successful Economy', in Christopher Clague and Gordon C. Rausser (eds), *The Emergence of Market Economies in Eastern Europe* (Cambridge MA: Basil Blackwell, 1992).

Olson, Mancur, 1997, 'Distinguished Lecture on Economics in Government, Big Bills Left on the Sidewalk: Why Some Nations Are Rich and Others Poor', *Journal of Economic Perspectives*, 10 (1997).

Olson, Mancur, Naveen Sarna and Anand V. Swamy, 'Governance and Growth: A Simple Hypothesis Explaining Cross-Country Differences in Productivity Growth', mimeo, Center of Economic Growth of the United States Agency for International Development (Washington DC 1997).

Pastor, Manuel, Jr., 'Latin America, the Debt Crisis, and the International Monetary Fund', in Jeffrey Frieden and David Lake (eds), *International Political Economy: Perspectives on Global Power and Wealth* (New York: St Martin's Press, 1991).

Payer, Cheryl, *The Debt Trap: The IMF and the Third World* (New York: Monthly Review Press, 1974)

Pejovich, Svetozar, 'The Market for Institutions versus Capitalism by Fiat: The Case of Eastern Europe', *Kyklos,* 47, 4 (1994).

Persson, Torsten, Gérard Roland and Guido Tabellini, 'Separation of Powers and Political Accountability', *Quarterly Journal of Economics,* 112, 4 (1997).

Piazolo, Daniel, 'Economic Growth through the Import of Credibility: The Importance of Institutional Integration for Eastern Europe', mimeo, *Kiel Institute of World Economics* (Kiel 1998).

Pohl, Gerhard, Robert Anderson, Stijn Claessens and Simeon Djankov, 'Privatization and Restructuring in Central and Eastern Europe: Evidence and Policy Options', World Bank Technical Paper, 368, World Bank (Washington DC 1997).

Polak, Jacques, *The Changing Nature of IMF Conditionality,* Essays in International Finance (Princeton NJ: Princeton University Press, 1991).

Polak, Jacques, 'The· IMF Monetary Model: A Hardy Perennial', *Finance and Development* (December 1997).

Przeworski, Adam, *Democracy and the Market. Political and Economic Reforms in Eastern Europe and Latin America* (Cambridge: Cambridge University Press, 1991).

Putnam, Robert, 'Diplomacy and World Politics: The Logic of Two-level Games', *International Organization,* 42, 3 (1988).

Qian, Yingyi and Barry R. Weingast, 'Institutions, State Activism, and Economic Development: A Comparison of State-owned and Township-Village Enterprises in China', in Masahiko, Aoki, Hyung-Ki Kim, and Masahiro Okuno-Fujiwara (eds), *The Role of Government in East Asian Economic Development. Comparative Institutional Analysis* (Oxford: Clarendon Press, 1997).

Radelet, Steven, 'Indonesia's Implosion', Harvard Institute for International Development, Internet Website: http://www.hiid.harvard.edu/pub/other/ indimp.pdf, visited 16 April 1999 (Cambridge MA 1998).

Radelet, Steven and Jeffrey Sachs, 'The Onset of the East Asian Financial Crisis', *Harvard Institute for International Development,* Internet Website: http://www.hiid.harvard.edu/pub/other/eaonset.pdf, visited 16 April 1999 (Cambridge MA 1998).

Radelet, Steven and Jeffrey Sachs, 'The East Asian Financial Crisis: Diagnosis, Remedies, Prospects', Harvard Institute for International Development, Internet Website: http://www.hiid.harvard.edu/pub/other/eaonset.pdf, visited April 1999 (Cambridge MA 1998).

Reissig, Rolf, 'Was wollen die Ostdeutschen', mimeo (Hamburg April 1997).

Remmer, Karen, 'The Politics of Economic Stabilization: IMF Standby Programs in Latin America, 1954—1984', *Comparative Politics,* 19, 1 (1986).

Rodlauer, Markus, 'The Experience with IMF-Supported Reform Programs in Central and Eastern Europe', *Journal of Comparative Economics,* 20, 1 (1995).

Roländ, Gerard, 'The Role of Political Constraints in Transition Strategies', CEPR Discussion Paper, 943, Centre for Economic Policy Research (London 1994).

Romer, Paul, 'Endogenous Technological Change', *Journal of Political Economy,* 98, 5 (1990).

Rona-Tas, Akos, Jan Buncak and Valentina Harmadyova, 'Post-communist Transformation and the New Elite in Slovakia', *Slovak Sociological Review,* 4, 1 (1999).

Root, Hilton L., *Small Countries, Big Lessons. Governance and the Rise of East Asia* (Hong Kong 1996).

Rose, Richard and Christian Haerpfer, 'New Democracies Barometer V: A 12-Nation Survey', *Studies in Public Policy*, 306, University of Strathclyde (Glasgow 1998).

Roubini, Nouriel (1999), 'What Caused Asia's Economic and Currency Crisis and Its Global Contagion?', New York University (Internet Website: http://www.stern.nyu.edu/~nroubini/asia/Asia Homepage. html#intro, visited 16 April 1999 (New York 1999).

Russett, Bruce and Harvey Starr, *World Politics; The Menu for Choice*, fifth edition (New York: Freeman, 1996).

*Russian Economic Trends*, various issues.

Sachs, Jeffrey, 'The Transition at Mid Decade', Economic Transition in Central and Eastern Europe, *American Economic Association Papers and Proceeding*, 86, 2 (1996).

Sachs, Jeffrey, 'International Economics: Unlocking the Mysteries of Globalization', *Foreign Policy* (Spring 1998).

Sachs, Jeffrey D. and Andrew M. Warner, 'Achieving Rapid Growth in the Transition Economies of Central Europe', Stockholm Institute of East European Economies, Working Paper, 116 (Stockholm 1996).

Sala-i-Martin, Xavier, 'I Just Ran Four Million Regressions', NBER Working Paper, 6252, National Bureau of Economic Research (Cambridge MA 1997).

Sarel, Michael, 'Nonlinear Effects of Inflation on Economic Growth', *IMF Staff Papers*, 43 (1996).

Schmieding, Holger, 'From Plan to Market: On the Nature of the Transformation Crisis', *Weltwirtschaftliches Archiv*, 129, 2 (1993).

Scholte, Jan A., 'The IMF Meets Civil Society', *Finance and Development*, 35, 3 (1998).

Schumpeter, Joseph, *Capitalism, Socialism, and Democracy* (London: Allen & Unwin, 1952).

Selowsky, Marcelo and Ricardo Martin, 'Policy Performance and Output Growth in the Transition Economies. The Transition from Socialism', *American Economic Association Papers and Proceedings*, 86, 2 (1996).

Slay, Ben, 'Rapid versus Gradual Economic Transition', *Radio Free Europe/Radio Liberty Report*, 3 (1994).

Stevens, Mike and Shiro Gnanaselvam, 'The World Bank and Governance', *IDS Bulletin*, 26, 2 (1995).

Stiglitz, Joseph E., 'Development Based on Participation – A Strategy for Transforming Societies', *Transition. The Newsletter About Reforming Economies*, 9, 6 (December 1998).

Streeten, Paul, 'Markets and States: Against Minimalism', *World Development* 21, 8 (1993).

Streeten, Paul, 'Governance', in M.G. Quibria and J. Malcolm Dowling (eds), *Current Issues in Economic Development. An Asian Perspective* (Hong Kong: Oxford University Press, 1996).

Taube, Gunter and Jeromin Zettelmeyer, 'Output Decline and Recovery in Uzbekistan: Past Performance and Future Prospects', *IMF Working Paper*, International Monetary Fund (Washington DC 1999).

*Transition*, various issues.

United Nations Development Programme, *The Shrinking State. Governance and Sustainable Human Development* (New York 1997).

United Nations Economic Commission for Europe, *Economic Survey of Europe in 1991–92* (New York 1992)

United Nations Economic Commission for Europe, *Economic Survey of Europe*, 2 (Geneva 1998).

Vachudová, Milada Anna and Tim Snyder, 'Are Transitions Transitory? Two Types of Political Change in Eastern Europe Since 1989', *East European Politics and Societies*, 11.1 (1997).

Van Brabant, Jozef, M. van, 'Lessons from the Wholesale Transformation in the East', *Comparative Economic Studies*, 35 (1993).

Wade, Robert, 'The Coming Fight Over Capital Controls', *Foreign Policy* (Winter 1998–99).

Wagener, Hans-Jürgen, *Zur Analyse von Wirtschaftssystemen. Eine Einführung* (Berlin: Springer–Verlag, 1979).

Wallich, Christine, 'What's Right and What's Wrong with World Bank Involvement in Eastern Europe', *Journal of Comparative Economics*, 20, 1 (1995).

Weber, Max, *Wirtschaft und Gesellschaft. Grundriss der verstehenden Soziologie* (Tübingen 1972/1921).

Weingast, Barry R., 'Constitutions as Governance Structures: The Political Foundations of Secure Markets', *Journal of Institutional and Theoretical Economics* 149, 1 (1993).

Weingast, Barry R., 'The Economic Role of Political Institutions: Market-preservıng Federalism and Economic Development', *Journal of Law, Economics and Organization* 11, 1 (1995).

Whitefield, Stephen and Geoffrey Evans, 'Political Culture Versus Rational Choice: Explaining Responses to Transition in the Czech Republic and Slovakia', *British Journal of Political Science*, 29, 1 (1999).

Wilson, James Q., *Bureaucracy. What Government Agencies Do and Why They Do It* (New York: BasicBooks, 1989).

Winiecki, Jan, 'Heterodox Stabilisation in Eastern Europe', EBRD Working Paper, 8, European Bank for Reconstruction and Development (London 1993).

Wolf, Holger C., 'Transition Strategies: Choices and Outcomes', mimeo (New York 1997).

World Bank, *Annual Report* (Washington DC various years).

World Bank, *World Development Report: From Plan to Market* (New York various years)

*The World Today*, various issues.

Zecchini, Salvatore, 'The Role of International Financial Institutions in the Transition Process', *Journal of Comparative Economics*, 20, 1 (1995).

# Index

Weingast, Barry R. 86
Wescott, Robert F. 53
Whitefield, Stephen 123
Wightman, Gordon 123
Wilson, James Q. 86
Winiecki, Jan 11
Wolf, Holger C. 51n, 52
Wolfensohn, James 14
World Bank 10, 13, 14, 24, 49, 51,

54, 56, 68–72, 81, 85, 86, 87, 88,
89, 92–106, 109

Young, Oran R. 12n

Zecchini, Salvatore 107n
Zeman, Miloš 120
Zettelmeyer, Jeromin 52n